HOW TO BE A TELEPI
By Steve Hou

HOW TO BE A TELEPHONE PSYCHIC

ACKNOWLEDGEMENTS

My grateful thanks to Diane Smurthwaite for her speedy and proficient proof reading, as well as for half a lifetime's friendship, guidance and support.

Thanks are due too, to Heather Bromley for inspiration and encouragement.

This book is dedicated to the hundreds of telephone psychics it has been my privilege to work with and I hope provide some input that has been of use.

BIOGRAPHY

Steve Hounsome has been involved in this field for over thirty years and has completed a wide variety of studies and activities in this time.

Steve holds qualifications in the following subjects –

* Progressive Healing
* Psychic Studies
* Esoteric Soul Healing
* Tarot
* Bach Flower Remedies
* Basic Counselling Skills

The training Steve has completed is as follows –

* One year Progressive Healing, Sanctuary of Progress
* One year Psychic Studies, Sanctuary of Progress
* Meditation - 2 years, private tutor
* Natural Magic, 1 year, Marian Green
* Ritual Magic, 1 year, The London Group
* Esoteric Soul Healing, 2 years, Isle of Avalon Foundation
* Bach Flower Remedies - Foundation Level Certificate
* Order of Bards, Ovates and Druids - 12 years, now initiated Druid member

Steve has also attended lectures and workshops too numerous to mention over the years and continues to add to his knowledge and experience by attending events as they occur and maintaining his own regular sacred practices in Meditation, Yoga and Chi Kung.

Steve has had articles published in many magazines, on a variety of the subjects he works in. These include Positive Health and Pagan Dawn, as well as many of the smaller titles produced in the Pagan and holistic communities.

Steve has appeared on TV, twice alongside Derek Acorah on Granada TV's show 'Psychic Livetime' and acted as examiner on the Living TV series 'Jane Goldman Investigates', overseeing the work of Michelle Knight who taught the Tarot to Jane.

Steve acted as advisor and consultant for the New World 'Music of the Tarot' CD, for which he also wrote the accompanying booklet.

Steve has had six books published –

* *Taming the Wolf: Full Moon Meditations*
* *Practical Meditation*
* *Practical Spirituality*
* *Tarot Therapy Vol. 1: Tarot for the New Millenium*
* *Tarot Therapy Vol 2: Major Arcana, The Seekers Quest*
* *Tarot Therapy Vol. 3: Minor Arcana, The Map of the Quest*

Steve has also produced his own unique card sets –

* *Chakra Affirmation Cards*
* *Tarot Therapy Affirmation Cards*

Steve has also produced a range of 15 highly-acclaimed Meditation and Development CD's, which you can see full details of in the Shop on this website.

Steve is currently working on his own 'Tarot Therapy' deck and plans to produce a major new workbook, called 'Sacred Living'.

Steve has taught in person across the South of England and by distance learning internationally. Apart from his own private events, Steve has taught at Adult Education Centres in Hampshire and was tutor of the 2-year Tarot course at the prestigious 'Isle of Avalon Foundation' in Glastonbury, Somerset. Steve has tested and trained psychic readers for some of the leading telephone psychic companies in the UK, working across the world.

Steve was a Founder Member and Secretary of the Professional Tarot Society and was also Secretary of the British Psychic Registration Board, although both these organisations are no longer in existence. Steve is now a member of the following organisations –

* Order of Bards, Ovates and Druids (Steve acts as mentor for those following their training programme)
* *Spiritual Workers Association*

* Tarot Association of the British Isles
* British Astrologers and Psychics Society
* Tarot Professionals

Though a member of these Groups, Steve's approach to spirituality is an eclectic one, as he feels that every path has something to offer. He reads widely on spiritual subjects and incorporates what he learns into his teaching, in its various forms. Steve feels that a sense of the sacred for each individual is vital to the maintenance of health and well-being and for the fulfilment of our potential, development and life purpose. More personally, Steve has a deep love of many forms of music, runs long-distance and cycles. He enjoys visiting sacred and natural sites, plays tennis, attends his local gym regularly as well as watching football, remaining loyal to his origins by supporting his home-town team, Brighton & Hove Albion. He is the father of two children, Dakota and Amber.

Contents

INTRODUCTION

Since the beginning of the 1990's the work of a psychic reader has changed dramatically. It used to be the case that working as a psychic, whether you used Tarot, crystal ball, mediumship or whatever to do your work, meant plying your trade at any number of 'psychic fayres', as well as touting for business wherever you could to attract clients which would invariably be seen at the reader's home.

Psychic Fayres were commonly held in the back or 'function' rooms of pubs and hotels and often left a great deal to be desired. Most psychics would agree these days that they work with a positive energy and such things as precipitous amounts of alcohol, smoking and loud noise that often came as part of the package with such venues, all contrived to make the job of the psychic harder.

It also meant travelling expenses for the reader, all of which ate into what were already limited profits, once the table fee had been paid, for the privilege of breathing in another's tobacco smoke and hearing so many voices competing for the prize of 'loudest psychic reading'! So many times over the years I found myself slogging from one railway station to another, bags in hand in the cold, wind and rain wondering why I was doing it and all for just a few pounds of profit!

The answer was that I did it because I love it – present tense. After 30 years of such work I still attend some fayres, although I am rather more select these days! However the proliferation in these events reached a peak at the end of the 1980's and has tailed off steadily since then and generally speaking, now only the good ones survive.

Another drawback of the psychic fayre is that they lacked privacy and for me this was a crucial aspect. It used to astound me that some people would strain to hear what was being said to a client of mine and were not even particularly discreet about it. My assumption was they wanted to suss out if I was any good or not, but then why not wait until I had finished and then ask the client what they thought!

With the advancement in telephone technology that came with the dawn of the 1990's a new opportunity arose for the jobbing psychic that gave an alternative to suffering train delays on a wet and windy Sunday afternoon. Now it was possible for the reader to give readings from home and for the client to have a reading from the comfort of their armchair with a cup of tea in hand.

Multiple line telephone systems meant it was possible for a system to be set up whereby the reader could be assigned a 'PIN' number as we know them nowadays, which was used to identify them. Incoming calls to any one of a large amount of numbers could then be directed to a specific PIN number, which the 'phone system would direct to that individual's telephone. Once answered the system would then connect customer to reader and away we went!

The introduction of 'premium rate services' for such calls meant that at a rate of what was then £1.50 per minute, there was scope for profit to be made by a company, once the reader had been paid an amount per minute and the cost of telephony and advertising was deducted.

It seems to be the case in human history that if we can do something we will, irrespective of whether it is a good thing or not. This being the case, companies soon sprang up that saw where a quick buck was to be made. By issuing a pack of Tarot cards and a book about them to anyone that applied they were slotted in an office next to many others 'readers' and told to keep the caller on the line for as long as possible.

The unfortunate customer then got a shock when their telephone bill arrived as this was the preferred method of charging at this time. Regulations of premium rate telephone services soon followed thankfully, then known as ICSTIS (now Phone Pay Plus) which stipulated, amongst others things, a maximum call length of 20 minutes, thereby limiting huge bills. The regulations will be examined in detail later but for now this began to shed some welcome light on what had become an established and growing industry free of any restraint and checks.

Thankfully the general public are not as stupid or gullible as many think and it was found that those who were clearly not in any way psychic soon began to fall by the wayside. Alongside this came the introduction amongst the more reputable telephone psychic companies of testing of psychics who applied to be readers and quality control checks, such as monitoring calls and offering feedback to readers.

Incidentally it was about this time that I entered the joyful fray, hence my credentials for writing this book. Although I have worked as a psychic for 30 years now, as well as teaching Tarot and related subjects and having published six books in this field, I also worked a few hours each week as a telephone psychic. This, I hasten to add, was after I had passed the stringent tests applied by the Company I worked for. I was then approached to take up the role of 'Reader Manager', meaning that I had responsibility for the acceptance or otherwise of the readers, as well as providing quality control and giving them feedback from listening to their calls. Some 13 years later, I am still doing this work, albeit with a different company. So this has given me a unique insight into the telephone psychic industry and this is why I am writing this book.

I am also writing the book in the hope that it may do something to help improve some aspect or standard and make the whole thing a better and more positive experience for reader and customer alike. In my experience I have found that some people, some good readers amongst them, think that it is a simply a case of turning up, logging on, picking up the 'phone when it goes, talking a bit, then logging off and taking the money. It is absolutely not and if you have picked up this book thinking that this will be a good wheeze and a means to make some money easily and quickly, think again. Please put the book back on the shelf and leave! Perhaps a different kind of line might suit you better!!

In actuality the work can at times be intense and hard. It requires a commitment to regular times, deft handling of people from all walks of life, sometimes with anger, certainly rudeness and deep issues to deal with, unsociable hours, unknown earnings and much more. With this however come the benefits of working from home, work in an area you have expertise in and love (these are both prerequisites on the part of the reader, as we shall see), the freedom of self-employment and a sense of job satisfaction that in my view at least, equals that of the highest possible.

This is because, for me, that this is not really work. For me it has over the years simply become part of who I am and what I have chosen to do with my life. It is an often unspoken aspiration for us to wish we could make a living from doing what we are passionate about, that continues to challenge us and demands the best from us and that deploys our creative potential and allows us true and lasting fulfilment. I am fortunate to be able to truly say a resounding yes to all of these. Make no mistake this has not come without blood, sweat and tears over the years, to the extent that some of us in our company once jokingly decided we should write into every employees contract that it be obligatory at some stage to have a 'hissy fit', resign and then retract it! In short when you are dealing with people's lives, this kind of occurrence cannot be avoided and nor should it.

I have stated above that my motivation in writing this book is to hopefully in some small way make a telephone psychic reading a better experience for reader and customer. I should perhaps also say that this is because I believe there is room for improvement and indeed there always should be. In dealing with other's lives this by default demands the very best of us as readers. Telephone psychic readings are not, apart from these days in law alone, an experiment to see how accurate we can be as psychics, but a vital means for the customer, to access some guidance, help and hope for problems they are trying to face, deal with and understand. Often it can be the case that people turn to psychics when other means of support have failed them. This is often because the psychic is able to access a level and degree of information unavailable by any other means.

Another part of my motivation for this book is also to hopefully inform and improve the image of the telephone psychic industry and to show that amidst the dross and drivel there are jewels and gems. Seek, as they say, and you shall find. In recent years there have been a number of media 'exposés' of fraudulent telephone psychics and whilst it is a good thing that these individuals have been 'outed' these showings also serve to taint the work of the rest of us and colour the image of the public as a whole and what they can expect when they call for a reading. Many callers are understandably guarded and almost expecting to be ripped off when they call, especially for the first time with a reader and as we shall see this immediately makes everything harder and potentially reduces the positivity and impact of the experience they may have.

So whether your interest is as a potential reader, customer with good or bad experiences or perhaps a company involved in this field, accompany me now as we seek those jewels, find some gems and polish them to become a shining light, twinkling on the sands of the telephone psychic world!

CHAPTER 1 – STARTING OUT

In this Chapter we will take a look at the process of becoming a telephone psychic, how it is done and what is needed.

First among these is of course, a psychic ability. This book will not teach you this or show you how you can develop your psychic skills, for that belongs elsewhere. However, there are many books, websites, courses and workshops, where you can get involved to your heart's content. This book is written under the proviso that you are reading it because you wish to become a telephone psychic or learn more about your existing line of work, and also that you already possess a developed and proven psychic ability.

I hope to show you how you can more easily adapt those skills to working by telephone effectively, but let me reiterate here that if you have obtained this book thinking you can simply get work without pre-existing expertise in this field, forget it. This line of work is not and never will be, for you.

It should also be made clear at the outset, that telephone psychic work is usually not for the fledging psychic or those who have just completed a 10 week 'psychic development' or Tarot course and now wish to start their careers. This is not to say that giving readings by 'phone requires you to be more advanced psychically, but in my experience it is best to acquire some practical and professional experience by giving readings in person and remotely, to build up your own and self-belief, before you throw yourself into the lion's den of the telephone psychic zoo!

Callers can be very demanding and exacting, wanting specifics and absolute spot-on information, and usually instantly, which we will deal with later, but it can be a very disheartening experience when you do not supply this within the first minute of answering the 'phone to be told how useless or worse, you are, or perhaps to have the 'phone put down on you while you are in mid-sentence, and labouring under the impression that you are doing well. I have known from these kind of scenarios, too many young psychics lose their nerve, confidence and trust in what has later been shown to be a good psychic ability and a genuine desire to use it positively for others. It is far better to wait and do readings, whether for a low fee, on an exchange basis or even free, to gain experience and confidence, as well as developing the back bone and thick skin required in a professional telephone psychic.

I have said this to a number of applicants over the years and have been a happy witness to some who have been humble and wise enough to follow these suggestions. They have returned after a suitable period of time, which varies from person to person, re-applied and demonstrated how much they have moved on by showing they are capable of dealing with the rude, abrupt denials and put downs they inevitably have received. They have then gone on to establish themselves successfully and productively.

So let us suppose you feel that you possess the necessary psychic skills and ability to be a professional telephone psychic. We will look shortly at what else is needed. However before we do that, let us ask ourselves why you wish to do this.

MOTIVATION

Examining our motivation is always a good thing to consider before any project we embark upon. There are different levels on which we may do our work. Over the years that the telephone psychic industry has evolved, there have only been a precious few that have really established this line of work as a full-time job, and made it their sole source of income and career.

The vast majority of telephone psychics work on a part-time basis and give readings online to blend with other areas of work in this field, whether this be readings for personal clients, teaching or attending 'psychic fayres'. Indeed it may be true to say that when asked, this same majority of readers prefer to give their readings in person rather than by 'phone. This in turn makes the approach to telephone psychic work as something of a 'necessary evil' to earn the required income. This I have to confess, is true in my case.

This does not in my case, and should not in anyone's case, change the actual approach to and regard for the work done or the readings given. This must always be the best that can be done. Given that we are dealing with people's lives in one way or another, this alone demands our utmost effort. Quite simply, if you cannot achieve this every day, you should not be working.

This is all said here to address the first motivation for the telephone psychic and really for almost all of us when it comes to our work, and that is money. The point is that we should admit that we work for the money, and indeed this work can pay well. There is nothing wrong with this of course and some are quite happy to show and allow this. However in my experience, a great many psychics are people who lead a spiritual life and as such, find that addressing the need for 'filthy lucre' distasteful.

Firstly, I would say that there is a need to be honest with yourself. I have experienced many readers who come across as spiritual and enlightened, claiming they are not concerned about the money, usually shortly before asking about the rate of pay! False spirituality immediately puts me off hiring them, as there is no place for falseness or ego-based spirituality when it comes to psychic work. There is nothing wrong with being paid for the work that you, do and it is very true to say that a client will value what they have been given if they have given something for it.

Equally however, we must also be on our guard against money being the sole aim of doing this work. If your reason for wanting to become a telephone psychic is to make money and only that, then think again. This is not to say that you will or will not, but there is a need to recognise that in this line of work, there are other issues to consider. As stated earlier, we are dealing with people's lives and the real issues with which they are confronted for which they are requesting our help. If we are only offering that help to make money from them there is something wrong with that equation. At its best it is exploitation and at its worst, simple abuse.

So why do you want to be a telephone psychic? Look to your conscience to give you an answer. There can be many different responses of course, but I do feel that chief among these should be a desire to help others, coupled with the knowledge that you possess, and the ability to do so with your psychic talents. We can add to this of course, the fact that there is income to be made from it and add to this the fact that we can make a living from doing what we love to do; this can be seen as a joy. It is taken as read that you do love giving psychic readings and are passionate about it. We will address this point elsewhere, but for now it is enough to say that without this level of motivation, this work is not for you. This passion will sustain you in what can be a trying, demanding, thankless and isolating job.

So from examining our motivation, we have perhaps seen that the work of a telephone psychic is done because we believe we are good at it, we can genuinely make a positive difference to peoples lives, it allows us an additional outlet for the work we cherish and it can help to pay our bills or perhaps earn some extra money. Work as a telephone psychic was never intended to be a full-time career path, to set us up for life and make lots of money easily and quickly. Now that is clear, do you still want to be a telephone psychic?

EXPERIENCE

Working on the assumption that your answer is yes, then we next need to look at what you need to have, to be a telephone psychic.

Foremost among the list of requirements is experience. This does not mean that you must have been an established, professional psychic for a number of years before you can be an effective telephone psychic. It does mean however, that at the very least, you need to have a level of confidence in your self and your readings, that goes beyond the merely acceptable 'competent'. People's lives require more than competency.

Many telephone psychics turn to this line of work as it is easier for them in their advancing years to do so, rather than trying to travel to fayres and the like. I know of telephone psychics in their 20's and in their 90's so there is a great scope here. One lady in her mid 90's I know, had failing eyesight and greatly impaired mobility, but possessed of a fantastic mind and vast astrological knowledge. Given that sleep did not come easily to her, she could frequently be found online at 2am, giving the most profound readings to those that came to her. Whenever I spoke to her she would cheerfully proclaim 'I'm still alive'! I'm not with that company now, so I don't know if this is still true, but I hope it is.

So we have established that you need experience to be a telephone psychic. It is simply not possible or good enough to buy a pack of Tarot cards and a book on their meanings and regurgitate these to your poor, unsuspecting callers. As we progress further with the advancement of our intuitive and psychic awareness, it is my experience that younger people are coming through with advanced psychic ability.

This can mean that some very good telephone psychics can come to the fore early in their careers and I do know of many in their 20's who succeed. That said, I have also experienced people, (I won't call them psychics), applying for work and literally reading out meanings from books in their reading for me! Those calls didn't last long I might add.

There can therefore be no hard and fast time at which any one individual can say that they have achieved the requisite experience to give psychic readings. It varies from person to person and it is really only you that will know for sure when you have achieved this level. We will talk elsewhere about the customers, the demands they make and the treatment you can expect from them, but for now, consider what this might be and if you have the necessary tools to cope with the very worst you can imagine.

Once you know and are certain that you have acquired the necessary experience at psychic work, then it is good and helpful to look at what else is required for this work. Here we need to turn to the subject of lifestyle and see how the work of a telephone psychic might blend with this and what adjustments you may need to make.

If part of your motivation is that you are looking for something nice and cosy, perhaps to make extra money while the kids are at school, then consider a little more. The majority of people in this country still work and do so during the daytime and on weekdays. This naturally means that more calls are made to telephone psychics in the evenings and at weekends. Of course there are calls during weekdays in the daytime, but if your only hours of work are going to be at these times, then you will make less money per hour and do less work.

LIFESTYLE

We need also to look at your own lifestyle and your natural body clock, so we can make best use of this for your work. Are you an early bird or a night-owl? Broadly speaking, people fall into one or the other bracket, so it makes sense to plan your working hours around this schedule. I have made it clear already that this work of necessity requires unsocial hours from you and here you can take advantage of this.

Just because you may be in the habit of rising at 5am, this does not mean that because the world seems quiet there will be no calls coming in. Telephone psychics are in demand right across the world, so given time differences, it's always night-time somewhere, and there are always people in need who are suffering and dealing with dilemmas. This is just as true at 2am as it is at 5am, so you can feel free to fit your existing lifestyle comfortably around your work.

You may need to think about other aspects of your lifestyle too. If you are someone who is in the habit of having a drink each evening then you will need to plan your working hours around this, or better still, cut out the alcohol on those nights. It should go without saying that you can absolutely not do any telephone psychic work if you have had a drink. Whilst I am on the subject, smoking while you are giving a reading is also forbidden. However careful you think you are being, the caller will hear this, which will sound totally unprofessional and indicate to them that your mind is elsewhere rather than on them and the reading.

You will also need to consider your living circumstances and the impact on anyone you live with both from their point of view and on your work. You will need quiet when you are working, the telephone will ring at 5am or midnight and so on. You may need to discuss the various issues with those in your household before you take up this work, especially given that it will need some unsocial hours from you. There are many levels of impact and some of these will be addressed elsewhere, but it really comes down to being realistic and sensible about the effect this will have on your particular living arrangements.

So it is sensible to ask yourself if you are willing to work when most others are not. Will you give up your Sunday morning lie-in or Saturday afternoon shopping, Friday night out and so on to do your work? This is when it is an advantage to be logged-on and working as more calls will come in at these times. The work of a telephone psychic is, in more senses than one, unsociable and this should be taken into account and accepted before you begin.

EQUIPMENT

Next on our agenda come the tools of the trade. You know now why you have chosen to do this work and also when, generally speaking, you will do it. Now we need to look at what you need to carry out your duties.

Obviously you will need the psychic necessities for the way that you work. If you are a Tarot reader you will need a Tarot pack; if you are work with a crystal ball, you will need one of these. This is very obvious of course, but it is mentioned here as it is worth giving some consideration to what psychic tools you will work with. As should be abundantly clear by now, giving psychic readings by telephone is different from face to face readings. Because of this, and because you will want to attract as wide a range of callers and as high a number of readings as possible, it is worth considering expanding your skill base to meet these requirements and demands.

We will look at the customers and their needs in the next chapter, which will help with this, but let us first look at you and what you offer. You may have given your readings using only the Tarot, but are you also a clairvoyant? If so are there other oracles or psychic tools that will help you deliver the best readings of which you are capable? It may well be worth the investment in trying these, as you may find that other tools and skills work better for you for telephone readings than they do in person. Equally, with the wealth of Tarot decks now in production, you may wish to search for the most suitable deck for your telephone readings. It may be that a different deck produces better results by 'phone for you than the one you are used to using for your personal readings. There is no substitute here for trial and error.

Many callers want definite 'yes or no' answers and for this a pendulum can be a real boon. Once you have looked at the why's and wherefore's of a callers situation, it may be that you can then turn to a pendulum to provide as definitively as possible a positive or negative answer for them.

If you are an astrologer, do you have the means to produce a caller's birth chart in seconds? This is what will be expected and the requirement for these readings by 'phone. It involves owning a good, professional astrology programme, of which there are many available now. It is pointless in this book, to recommend any specifics for the tools you use, both because this is a personal choice and by the time this is published, what is recommended will have been superseded by something else! In the case of astrologers, what is important before you begin giving readings online, is that you are fully familiar and conversant with the inner workings of your chosen programme. Ensure that you can access all the information you might ever require during a reading, and are able to cope with even the most unexpected question a caller might ask. You can be sure that if you have thought of the possibility of someone asking it, there will be a caller who surely will, and more besides! You cannot allow yourself even the remotest possibility of having to admit to a caller that you do not know how to find that information in your programme. Not only will you sound like an amateur who does not know what they are doing, but it will also mean a customer lost, along with any recommendations they might have made to others.

Apart from the necessary psychic tools you will need, as we can recall and define them, there are other requirements necessary for the professional fulfilment of your duties. Perhaps first among these is a timer. Many of your calls will be for a specific amount of time, ranging possibly from just 20 minutes to an hour or more. We will look at the dynamics of this later, but for now it is enough to know that you need to pace and structure the reading, not to fill up the time, but to ensure that you are in control of the process, and able to fully address all the callers needs and questions.

A basic kitchen timer will enable you to this, letting you see at a glance how long you have left on each call. Most timers, for the cost of a few pounds, have a digital display. Many psychics in their personal readings are used to either letting the reading take as long as it needs or working to a time structure, but routinely going over this time. This may be great for appearing generous, but this does not work the same way for telephone readings.

For calls via a premium rate line, which will be explained later, there is a time limit applicable, after which you are cut off. For booked calls the same applies, and usually, following a warning message, the call is also terminated. The best professionals will always be bringing the calls to a rounded conclusion and summary during the last two minutes of a call, and a timer is invaluable at facilitating this.

There are other tools and equipment you may need to consider as well. If you are a card reader of any kind, you will obviously need a suitable surface on which to place your cards. This will mean a table and possibly a cloth which allows you to see the cards clearly. You will need to ensure you have adequate space, and all the things you might need during a reading to hand.

Some readers combine astrology with card readings so in this case, you will need to consider easy and comfortable access to your pc screen. You will need to place your timer where you can see it as well as having a glass of water always available to ease the dry throat that you will get, and usually at the most inconvenient times! This needs to be placed somewhere that you will not knock it flying, especially if, as in my case, you can become somewhat animated with the reading and your arms start to gesticulate wildly! Soggy Tarot cards do not shuffle well!

Your shifts may, and can sometimes be busy, with almost back to back calls, so it is sensible and prudent to gather all that you think you might need before you begin. Certainly you may have time between calls to make a coffee, but there is nothing worse than having to dash across the house to grab the 'phone and then start to your call somewhat breathless, leaving the caller wondering what is going on! Seriously, if you do not sound prepared and calm, you have an immediate uphill battle to gain their trust and confidence, and this, as you will see later, is very important.

Next is your choice of venue for your readings. You will need a place that enables you to do your readings comfortably and effectively. This may sound obvious but I have known readers who have done their readings lying propped up in bed. Whilst this does not necessarily detract from the quality of a reading, it certainly does not add to it, and does not lend itself to the professionalism that is required.

In choosing where you will work from choice, this should be done with exactly that in mind – work. Whilst it is not the same as going out to work in an office, bank, supermarket etc. you should have the view that when you log on to give readings, you are going to work and be prepared and set-up accordingly, So when it comes to where you will work, it is ideal, if at all possible, to have a separate room that serves as your working room. Having this luxury enables you to 'go to work', do your thing, then come out, shut the door and leave it behind, which as we shall see is important on many levels.

For many of us however, such luxurious living arrangements are not possible, so the requirement then is to have an area set aside which is dedicated to your work space, whether this doubles up as your dining table or whatever. When the times comes to log on, you can then 'convert' it to your working space, with all the tools and equipment you require set up and ready.

Foremost among your requirements is to look at your seating arrangements. A good sized table to lay out your cards, house the computer, candles and so on, is clearly the first thing needed. Next is a good chair, which will offer you the correct access to your table as well as support for your posture. You may spend many hours in this chair, so it is vital you give due consideration, and if necessary money, to being able to sit comfortably, if you are to avoid back, neck, hand or any other ache.

If you live in a household with other people, this will also need to be considered. Whilst your caller may, and sometimes will, have all kinds of noise in the background, you are a professional and you cannot have any background noise distracting you or your caller from your work and the reading. It is surprisingly easy to hear what you may think are quiet noises in the background on the other end of the 'phone. I have in my time, come across readers who have had budgies and canaries singing, a collection of clocks chiming, and even been heard to go to the toilet mid-reading!

Companies will not tolerate this and customers will complain, so if you live with other people, it will need to be understood that no disturbances or audible noises are acceptable while you are working. This will include pets – there is little more unpleasant to someone paying £1.53 per minute for a telephone call, than to have two minutes or more of this drowned out by the barking of the readers Alsatian or whatever. You would not expect this if you visited a solicitor or estate agent, so why should you as a psychic?

You may also need to think about your telephone, perhaps your primary piece of equipment for this work. Where will it be placed and is it going to cause a hazard? It is all too easy unfortunately, to forget about the wire you think you have placed out of reach, to somehow reach out and wrap itself around your foot the moment you move. Not only can you fall, but that wire is expert at grabbing the phone from you and flinging it across the room, which does not help your caller just when you are explaining to them how they can turn their life around!

An essential edition is a telephone with a headset. As already stated you may well spend long hours on your 'phone and you will undoubtedly get into the habit of propping the 'phone between your shoulder and your ear. The only way to keep it there is to tilt your head. This will soon create neck ache, headache, ear ache and potentially serious back problems. The easy answer to this is to get a telephone with a headset. There are many available now that come with a headset socket, which allows you to unplug this if you wish, and they do not cost a great deal.

An advantage with a headset is also, of course that it leaves your hands free, which is very . . . well, handy, if you are a Tarot reader. Again, some readers feel it is acceptable to tell the caller they'll be 'back in a minute' then comes a thud as the 'phone goes down while they deal out cards, then grab the 'phone again. You may do 3 or 4 different Tarot spreads in a reading and this scenario is to be avoided.

Having a headset allows for greater comfort, which I have also found allows for greater involvement with your caller. Somehow having their voice coming closer to you and your being able to move about if you wish and express yourself with your hands, despite them not being able to see this, allows you to feel and be more involved. The voice, as you will see, is all important when it comes to making your psychic connection with each person.

So the only real essentials, which if lacking, do not allow you to do this job, are a place to read, somewhere to lay out your cards etc., a place to sit and a telephone, preferably with a headset. If you choose to lay your cards on a cloth that is fine, along with any other more decorative items you may choose for whatever reason. Many readers will have a crystal or two near to them to enhance the vibration of their space, may light incense when they begin work or play quiet, relaxing music in between (not during) calls. Whatever you feel will aid your readings is fine, so long as it does not distract from your focus and attention and what the caller hears.

So now that we have established when and where you will work, we can turn our attention a little more to the work itself. We will look at readings and their dynamics in a further chapter but for now we will look at how you attract business and calls to yourself.

As stated previously, the majority of psychics prefer to give their readings in person. However the tricky part of that is attracting enough clients. This is the great advantage of telephone psychic lines: they provide the clients for you, This is not to say that millions of them don't appear out of nowhere of course, and a great deal of effort can be made on your behalf by the companies, where there is much competition to attract deals and contracts with the top magazines and newspapers.

I have found that many readers tend to ignore or forget that although their preference is not to give readings by telephone, that by doing so they can make good money, working from home with no expense and inconvenience of travel, doing something they have chosen to do and love, rather than having to work out of necessity in some dusty office, stacking the shelves of the local supermarket or cleaning the local school. Better then to take the attitude of being realistic with yourself, honour the company you work with and thank them for helping to allow you this lifestyle and income, which provides you with enough clients to allow you to do what you do.

That however, is not really your concern, but you can help yourself in a number of ways by providing and having readily available, the information a company will require. In reality the only people who, in effect, are in competition with you, are the other readers. Being a largely genuine mob, there is very little cut throat activity and a communal spirit exists amongst readers which is essentially helpful. So what is required is that you place and keep your focus on yourself and be the best that you can be. As stated previously, the business and ethics of giving readings, requires this level of commitment on behalf of your clients and their lives.

Once a company has accepted your services (we will look at the recruitment shortly), it will be necessary for you to have prepared some information from which, they will be able to best promote you. I have found that many psychics do not deal easily and willingly with the 'ways of the world' but these are basic requirements that must be met and adhered to, if you wish to work with a reputable company. Obtaining the following information has been on many occasions like getting the proverbial blood from a stone and I have at times, given up as it has simply not been worth the time and effort and is an indicator that the reader will not be reliable or professional. So bear this in mind from the start, which is the reason that I mention this at this point.

Most companies will have their own website on which they will feature a profile of each reader, which will be available to their callers. For this, they will need some written information from you and it is helpful to prepare this in advance before applying to companies, as this will not only give a professional image from the start but will also show your serious intent and, if my experience is anything to go by, will also set you apart from the pack, which is never a bad thing in any sense in which it may apply.

Your profile may need to cover the following areas -

DEVELOPMENT AND HISTORY – This should cover all training you have completed that is relevant to your work as a reader. This can (and should), include counselling training and any therapeutic qualifications you have gained, as well as more specific training, with dates and the name of the institution or person studied at or with. You should include here evidence of ongoing training, which if you are a professional working psychic needs to be apparent. This may be sitting in a psychic development circle or some such, but it will create the best impression if you are able to demonstrate that you are aware you do not 'know it all', and are open to the idea that you can still learn. I have experienced readers who have told me when arranging test readings from them, that they have been a reader for 30 years and will clearly pass any test. Such arrogance is immediately off putting to my mind. Do not be like them, but have a little humility, humanity and openness.

Lastly include in your development and history details of where you have provided readings, with dates, to demonstrate the experience you have. If you have worked for other telephone psychic companies, state this clearly and include any pseudonym you may have used as well as the PIN number allocated to you. Do not think you can get away with lying or making anything up, as some people do on CV's – they will be obvious to the trained eye and remember that you are dealing with psychics here and we can spot a liar a mile off!

SKILLS – This should be a paragraph clearly explaining what you do and how you do it. Remember that what you write for your profile will be seen by your customers and it is quite likely that the majority of these will not know the difference between a pendulum and a birth chart. So avoid jargon and explain succinctly any terms that anyone may not identify. The basics, you can assume will be understood, such as Astrology, the Tarot and Medium ship, but it is wise not to assume more knowledge than this.

It is fair to say that many psychics have trained or studied in a good many of the different psychic disciplines and modalities in the years they have been operating as psychics. Consequently they (note deliberate use of that term here!) can be a little too eager to tell anyone who will listen and some who may not, their list of achievements and areas of expertise. However it is all too easy to come across in a profile such as this, as a 'jack of all trades', implying by this of course that you are a master of none.

This is not to say that you should not mention all that you have done, for it will no doubt have cost you much in terms of finance, time and probably blood, sweat and tears, if my own experience is anything to go by. What can be best for your profile is to first and foremost make clear the main focus of your work e.g. 'I use the Tarot as the focus of my readings, having studied and worked with it for over 30 years'. You might then add later something along the lines of 'to complement my work with the Tarot I work with numerology (the science of numbers), as well as clairvoyance and on occasions a scrying mirror, to look into your past lives.

Following this process, what you finish with is one or two paragraphs at most, that give the reader swiftly and clearly, a good idea of what they can expect when they have a reading with you, what their reading will contain, what will happen and what they can expect to get out of it.

TESTIMONIALS – Lastly, many telephone psychic companies now have on display comments or testimonies from customers who have had readings with you. The ethics and usefulness of this is open to debate, but for now it is wise to gather together a number of

testimonies to accompany
your application or have available when requested.

If you do not have any testimonies from previous customers it will be
necessary to contact some to request them. Any and all testimonies
provided should be fully and completely genuine; there can be no
exceptions to this. Anything lacking in authenticity will not carry the
energy of truth with it and this will soon show up for what it is and
business will be lost as a result.

Testimonies do not need to be long; a paragraph at most and some
companies may want just one juicy 'one-liner' from you. When you
do present your testimonies do read them over beforehand.
Correcting grammatical and spelling mistakes is acceptable, but
changing the content is not. Every testimonial should be
accompanied by the persons name and their location. Anonymity is
vital here, so the name given, although it must be genuine, can be a
first name only, or initials. The location given need only be a town.

As the reader, you should also retain a copy of all the testimonials
you present, so that you can produce these if required for any
reason.

WHAT'S IN A NAME?

As a telephone psychic, quite a lot is in your name. As far as
possible, use your real name. Every telephone psychic company
that I know of or have seen, uses only the first name for a reader
and they do protect the reader's privacy well. The systems used do
not permit any direct access to you at all.

Firstly the question of authenticity arises as soon as we consider
using a different name. Your name carries your energy, assigned to
you at birth, for life. You may have made a conscious decision to
change your name by deed poll or marriage at some point, and this
of course is fine, but so far as is acceptable to you, your first name
is the best one to use, as this is who you are. The telephone psychic
industry has suffered enough bad publicity and suspicion without it
being added to in however small a way.

That said, that is the ideal and for many different reasons may not
be possible. Many psychics are also actors and they cannot mix the

two. Others have jobs or professions where it is wise, if not required, to not be seen on psychic based websites of any kind, such is the prejudice that can still exist in some poor people's minds. I know of telephone psychics who are teachers, work in social services and so on, who cannot use their own names for fear of reprisal by individuals or the 'powers that be'.

It is also best to avoid silly-sounding 'new age' names such as 'Crystal Silver Cloud', 'Destiny Divine' and so on. It is obvious, unless you are very unfortunate, that this is not your real name and people simply do not take these seriously. However genuinely implied, your spiritual intent might be by using a name such as this, you should remember that the majority of people who call telephone psychic lines do so because they want help with their relationship, career, kids and money. They are real people with real, everyday lives who do not care one jot about how enlightened you are or might wish to appear to be, So get real, get grounded and call yourself John or Julie, if that's who you are.

Many psychics have adopted what is in effect a 'stage-name' from the outset of their psychic careers and have built up a regular following and good reputation using this. That being the case, it makes sense to use this. I do not think this deducts from authenticity since it is used with correct intention and has always been the name used for that person in doing this work.

PICTURE PERFECT

The primary method of promotion for the majority of telephone psychic companies is websites, as is the case with all things of value (and many that are not), nowadays. Alongside this, there are also printed adverts appearing in the various newspapers and magazines, to which the different companies pitch viciously against one another to win the prized agreement. These adverts may often contain a 'featured reader' detailing their profile, a quote saying how wonderful their reading was, from a valued customer, and a photo of the reader. These adverts can be a primary source of attracting calls and business to you and it is therefore in your interest to provide as good quality a picture as possible.

Over the years I have been sent pictures of readers to accompany their profile, from holidays, weddings, evenings in the pub and so on! These usually have other people in them, can be blurred (especially the pub ones), and have 'red eye' when taken with a flash. Amazingly, they fully expect these to be acceptable as a professional, promotional shot of themselves to attract callers just to them, rather than any other reader.

When I explain that these kind of images are not up to the task required, there is usually some grumbling and moaning about not having any other photo, some self-disparaging remarks about them not being model-like (how many psychics are also models – I've met one in 30 years!), and the inconvenience of it all. It is at this point that I begin to wonder if I should have taken on this particular reader.

As the owner of one telephone psychic website said to me 'There is no substitute for a good quality, well-lit, picture of the reader smiling', and he is quite right. He himself is a well established and respected reader. If you cannot be bothered to obtain a good quality photo for your business, then do think again if this is the right outlet for you,

Many readers also provide a photo, or image, of themselves taken in their local passport booth. This produces a common-looking 'mug shot,' that inevitably leaves them looking more like a criminal than a professional psychic, no matter how well-dressed and smiling they try to be.

There really can be no excuse for not having a photo shoot done at a professional photographic studio. This is not as expensive as you would think and with the technologies possible now, you will come out looking just wonderful (all hail 'Photoshop'!). A good photographer will work with you and guide you on how to look for your particular, individual appearance as well as how to pose and so on. If you let yourself go a little, a professional photo shoot can be a very enjoyable experience and an opportunity to indulge in a little self-flattery and ego boosting when you see the results. Far from being just one costly photo, most photographers will supply you with multiple images for you to use, which can suit a variety of purposes, not just your telephone psychic website profile.

The cost of course is also tax deductible, so put your objections aside, hang your embarrassment up at the door and get thee to the photographer!

If you still find yourself resisting this, spend a little time sampling through the various telephone websites that you will have no trouble in finding. Wade through the hundreds of psychic profiles and observe your instinctive and immediate responses to the images you see. Put yourself in the customer's place, who is someone about to spend a goodly amount of money they perhaps cannot really afford on a reading. Would you go with the reader who has a slightly blurred, fuzzy look to them with red eyes like something from a 'Doctor Who' episode, or the one who is looking at the camera, smiling and well-defined? I know which one would appeal to me as suggestive of a good quality reading, and there would be no suggestion of time-travelling police boxes!

FINDING A JOB

Now that you are the proud possessor of your ready and waiting workspace and equipment, profile, testimonial and photo, all that remains is to get a job!

In my experience, many readers think this is easier than it is, but this can although maybe should not be the case. It is true that in the 1990's it would be enough to simply call a company, tell them you are a psychic and the job was yours. However, while there may unfortunately be a tiny number of those companies still operating, the vast majority of telephone psychic companies now operate good policies and ethics and you cannot simply walk into a job.

Regardless of how long you many have been giving psychic readings it cannot be stressed how important it is that you gain some experience of giving readings by telephone before you apply for a job doing just that. Apart from it being simple common sense, my experience has been that the very worst kinds of applicants are those that think they are great.

One of the greatest enemies a professional psychic has is their ego. Pride in your work and professionalism is one thing, but thinking you are the worlds greatest psychic with the best reputation ever, immediately sets you up for failure on many levels. This attitude of 'it's all beneath me,' puts me off more than anything when I have someone apply for work with this attitude. When I inform them that we will require at least two test readings to decide if they are right for us and indeed, if we are right for them, I am usually treated to a verbal history of all their experience, magazine articles, radio/TV shows, praise, triumphs, signs and wonders, so that by the end of it I am expecting nothing less than instant enlightenment from their reading. These people usually conclude their tirade by telling me of course, if I still require them to submit to a test reading, that it will be no problem for them, implying the assumption on their part that of course they will pass and be accepted. I immediately think, that I may have a problem here and that if they don't live up to their fantastic self-billing I am going to be rather disappointed. This almost always turns out to be the case. When I tell them that they have not been accepted, I am usually told that they knew this anyway and their Guide has told them that this is not the right company for them. Too true!

So, do not be like that. Leave your ego behind; it has no place in the psychic world, regardless of how good you have been told you are and what a bright future you have. If you want a good job with a reputable company, you can and should be expected to be tested. If you baulk at this then consider why, and most likely accept that you are not yet ready for this work. Humility is good but different to confidence, and you need a good dollop of both if you are going to be a professional telephone psychic.

For those that feel a test is not really necessary or profess nerves before they start, I say two things, Firstly that it is good. In reality they should feel some nerves, as it is a good indication that they are taking it seriously and also that it means something to them and it matters, just as it should. Secondly I explain that although the experience of being tested is not a particularly pleasant one as no-body likes it, every reading should really be regarded as a test. I remind them that the readings they give are real, that the people they give them to are real, with real problems and issues, for which they seek a reading, and in life there is no such thing as a test; there is only experience. I also tell them that we are on their side, we will be wanting more readers or we would not be talking to them and testing them, and if they cannot handle it when we want them to succeed, they certainly would not be able to cope with any of the more challenging or difficult callers that can and will come their way, let alone the nice, responsive ones!

So if you can understand and accept all of that, let us now look at how you get the job you want as a telephone psychic, and guide you through the testing process.

It is not the approach of this book to recommend any one Company above another or to suggest that one is better another. At the time of writing, there are still a good many companies trading and the reader can, to some extent, pick and choose with whom they place their trade.

A good internet search with a little time and patience, will soon give you the required links to contact by telephone the different companies. If you search for telephone psychics you will certainly find many sites offering readers, but the links to working as a reader can be hard to find. Include 'jobs' or 'working' in your search, which will save you much time and anguish.

The other route you may choose is to search the ubiquitous adverts offering readings. There are two things to be aware of if you choose this route, Firstly, consider the adverts you are looking at and where you see them. The majority of daily newspapers will have at least half a page of small box adverts offering readings of all kinds (and many other calls besides!). It should be considered that these are often reflective of the 'lower' end of the market of telephone psychic work, and that the company you approach may be reflective of where they place their advertising.

A further look in these publications will usually show you a column that is the 'officially approved' company with which the publication has chosen to place their product. This means that the psychic company will have had to meet their sometimes stringent standards of business and product quality (i.e. good readings), to win the contract. Competition can be fierce for these companies and they will be prepared to go to some lengths to secure the best readers.

You may also benefit from purchasing magazines that specialise in the psychic and spiritual fields, as these will also contain adverts for telephone psychic companies. A little time spent leafing through the titles available will soon allow you to see which companies advertise where, and so the kind of clientele they will attract. You will also be able to see those companies that advertise in more than just one publication and see the type, quality and size of adverts that they place. This will all help to give you a good idea of the kind of company each one is, plus some idea of the budget they spend to attract business. This will directly impact on the amount you can earn.

Do bear in mind with this, that those companies that advertise in only the more spiritually inclined magazines, may indeed attract more of the callers for whom you would ideally like to read, those being people that want guidance with the nest stage of their spiritual development. But even a brief experience in this field will have told you that such folk are not often disposed to call telephone psychic lines, and there are precious few of these compared to those that will call to find out if they are going to meet someone new, or if their boyfriend is coming back to them. Be realistic!

To contact companies through the advertising route you may need a magnifying glass! By law companies advertising premium rate telephone services, of whatever kind, are required to give, alongside the price of such calls, the name of the company and an address. This will appear in tiny, black print beneath the colour advert itself. This is not because the company is trying to hide their identity but simply trying to give as much space to their advert as possible. The company name may often be initials only, as an abbreviation, and the address a PO Box, used to simply receive mail.

It is perfectly acceptable to send a C.V. or application to that address, although it is not the best approach. The vast majority of us have access to the internet these days (and bear in mind that an increasing number of companies have this as a pre-requisite for their readers), so by searching the name and address given in the advert, a more direct approach can then be made.

APPLICATIONS

When making your first approach to a telephone psychic company it may be wise to first enquire if they are accepting readers at this time. A polite and above all professional approach will immediately set you apart from the crowd and believe me, with the standards set so far in this regard, this is easy. The vast majority of psychics seem to find it hard to function in a professional and acceptable manner in the more grounded business world of today. This is not to say that you must immediately abandon all sense of individual identity and conform to a world of automatons – I know that most psychics delight in their sense of individuality and separateness from the 'normal' world. In this you can rest easy – it is your individual psychic qualities that the company wants, not to absorb your identity into some gigantic machine!

However, the ability to communicate clearly, politely and professionally will have a big impact from the start. I continue to be dismayed at the standard of English in applications, along with the attitudes displayed by so many readers throughout the application and testing process. This tends to range from the ego-based 'of course you'll give me a job, I'm so good' approach to the totally disorganised 'oh I didn't write the time of the test down. Is it any wonder that I have a measure now of 'psychic or psycho'?

By now, if you have followed the suggestions given, you should have a C.V. and a profile with photo ready and waiting. A good and professional initial enquiry can then introduce you, ask whether they are currently accepting readers or have vacancies (demonstrating your awareness of how the industry works), and give a brief sentence or two describing your work and previous experience, also attaching your CV for further information.

A suggested sample may look something like this -

Dear Sir/Madam

Re: Working as a Telephone Psychic

I am writing to enquire as to whether you are currently accepting readers to your telephone psychic lines.

I have been working as a professional reader for 10 years, both at public events, privately and by telephone. My specialist areas are with the Tarot and clairvoyance and also a little medium ship.

I have attached my CV giving you full information of my experience and qualifications.

I trust that you will find this of interest and look forward to hearing from you,

Yours faithfully

Fred Blogs.

Your names, address, email and telephone numbers should then appear here.
As stated before, this alone will set you apart from almost all others making approaches in this field. I for one would immediately feel I wanted this person, as long as their readings matched up to their presentation so far.

A TESTING TIME

Next are the test readings. Any company concerned with the quality of their product, in this case telephone psychic readings, would require their applicants to be able to prove their ability and suitability for what they offer, so it is best if you are fully prepared and indeed expect this.

As mentioned previously, some readers baulk at this prospect and apply various means and methods to see if they can be avoided. These range from the 'I've been reading for 30 years why do I need to be tested' to 'I don't work at my best when I know it's a test, so it's artificial'. To all these I say that your client's life is not artificial, there are no rehearsals in life, only experience. Given this, every reading is therefore really a test, and should be treated as such. Also of course, this is a job interview, albeit one of a slightly different nature. You would not expect to simply walk into a prospective employer and be given the job straight away, so why should this be any different?

So the attitude when told that you will be required to provide test readings should be one of welcome and ready acceptance, perhaps even mentioning that this is a good indication that the company cares both about its product, its readers and above all its clients.

Many companies will require two test readings and indeed so they should. Remember that callers can either use a premium rate line for their reading or book a longer call and pay by debit or credit card. Premium rate calls are limited by law, at the time of writing to a maximum of 20 minutes. Booked calls can be set by the company and most have a maximum duration of one hour. For this reason you may be required to provide an initial reading of 20 minutes and if this is deemed acceptable, a longer one of perhaps 45 minutes.

This will be arranged with you either by email or phone and an appointment booked. Should you receive a call asking you to provide the first reading there and then, without prior notice and if you are able to, it is perfectly acceptable and in my view, preferable, for you to ask for a few minutes to prepare, to gather your equipment and attune yourself psychically. Any company not recognising the need for you to do this is not the right one to work for, since it shows a lack of understanding and awareness of psychics and their work, from the outset.

When an appointment is arranged it is important that you keep it and are properly prepared for it. This may seem obvious but so many times I have found readers unprepared or simply not available when I call at the agreed time. Even if they do then provide the reading at a later time, they have already gained a black mark against them, since it shows they are not fully professional and may be unreliable when it comes to logging on at the agreed time for their work.

It should of course go without saying that you should be prepared to give of your best in both or all of your test readings, and do so for as long as required. Some readers display a reluctance to give readings for free but again, this is misplaced and unacceptable. An attitude of humility and professional compliance is required instead.

Most companies will require test readings of varying duration. The first is most commonly a 20 minute reading, since as mentioned this is the maximum duration allowed by law on any premium rate service. The second will usually be a longer reading, of perhaps 40 to 45 minutes. This is usually done so the company can be assured that you can provide continuing quality of information for a longer, booked call. They, and indeed you, need to know that you do not run out of steam or information or that you come across as just filling up time. Telephone psychic readings are expensive and apart from any other issue, it would be morally and ethically wrong to just string someone along for part of their reading when you have nothing useful left to say. Any good psychic working professionally should be able to give a top quality reading for a minimum of an hour without even blinking.

During your test readings it is a good idea to monitor the time and gear your reading accordingly. When you reach 20 minutes, round the reading off and your tester will then give you feedback. It can be useful to mention that you had plenty more left to say, but concluded the reading, as the 20 minutes was up. For the second test the same applies with regard to timing and it is vital in all readings, test or otherwise, that you do not refer to the length of time left as this only serves to show that you will just keep talking to fill up the time, rather than being involved and immersed in the reading.

The attitude here really needs to be that you have only 20 minutes to do a reading, so it is a challenge to get everything in. However before we stray into the whys and wherefores of giving readings prematurely, let me refer you instead to Chapter 2 where details and guidance for giving readings by telephone follow. This should be read and absorbed before you make any applications.

THE DOTTED LINE

To my knowledge, without exception all telephone psychics are self-employed. Whatever company you work with, will therefore require you to sign a self-employed contract to confirm this. Some readers may baulk at this but such officialdom must, these days, be observed. Gone are the days of cash in hand and under the counter payments!

The contracts can vary in form from a simple one page document testifying to your self-employed status, to many pages of 'legalese'. Either way you have no choice but to sign on the required dotted line. Any reputable company will not be seeking to 'rip you off' in anyway and any company lacking in the legal requirements and clarity that such contractual obligations bring, should not be worthy of your time and attention regardless of any other considerations.

The contract you sign may and indeed should, specify the amount of remuneration payable to you – I have avoided the terms 'pay', 'wage' or 'salary' here, since this implies an employed status and you are highly unlikely to find any company or its contracts using such terminology lest anyone attempt to ascertain they have been employed. Such a travesty would immediately make that company liable to pay all its readers tax and national insurance payments, which would bankrupt them overnight! So, self-employed you will be and self-employed you will remain!

The actual rate of payment made to you will usually be termed 'per minute' and this can vary a great deal. At the time of writing I know of some companies that pay a woeful and frankly insulting 12 pence per minute for part of some calls, whilst the highest I have yet come across is a healthy 50p per minute. What you earn of course will depend on the number and frequency of calls that you receive along with the number of hours you are prepared or able to work. Most companies will offer a rate per minute somewhere between these two extremes, and in mid-2013, when this is being written, this will be approximately 33 pence.

You can usually expect to be paid on a monthly basis, although I do know of one company that pays weekly but they appear to offer a reduced per minute rate for the privilege! The main reason for monthly payment is that companies usually receive their income from the calls monthly. It can be a common misconception that 'office staff' and the telephone psychic companies themselves are all on massive salaries and making a huge amount of profit.

This is actually not the case, especially in these days of increasing competition between the companies, for what is actually a limited customer range, albeit one of a high number. The costs involved are large, including the aforementioned office personnel and not least is the equipment and telephony costs which amount to the majority of what must be paid. In addition, the governing body for premium rate telephone services have only increased the permissible cost of calls once in over 15 years, whilst all other costs have risen far beyond this amount. So bear this in mind, that despite an amount of £1.53 per minute coming in from every call that is taken, this business is not an easy way of 'making a quick buck' or even a very big buck! It can however be a good and noble way to help you pay your bills, or make extra money and allow you to fulfil your ambitions to help people as a psychic.

Most companies will send you a monthly statement of the amount you have earned, which should always be retained, as it will be needed when it comes to completing your end of year accounts (see Chapter 4 for further information on this). The trendy term for this statement is currently a 'self-bill invoice', which does not mean that it is a bill for you to pay, but is in effect the bill you would send to the company. However, they have saved you the bother.

So, now that you have passed your tests, completed your profile, provided a photograph and signed the paperwork, you are all set to begin walking the weird and wonderful path that is the work of the telephone psychic! As I have often said, it's better than working for a living! By this I mean that for me it really is unlike work, since 'being a psychic' is and in my view, really should be a way of life; something that is part of who you are and what you do, rather than just your work – a vocation rather than a profession if that does not sound too grand a way of putting it.

CHAPTER 2 – THE READINGS

Giving a telephone psychic reading is so much more than just chatting to someone for a while. Indeed it can also be a different proposition to a face to face reading in as much that the dynamics are different, even if the content can be similar. Let us now explore those dynamics a little and observe some of the regulatory do's and don'ts of telephone psychic readings.

It should be abundantly clear by now that this is a professional job requiring the same approach and attitude. This applies to each and every shift that you work and to each and every reading that you give on that shift. It therefore becomes implicit that you prepare yourself fully before each and every shift, so that you can ensure you work to the very best of your ability in an appropriate, safe and effective way.

If you are an established psychic of any kind then you may think that you are aware all there is to know with regard to giving readings. That may be the case but that does not mean that there is no room to learn a little more. Over the years I have had dealings with hundreds of telephone psychics of all ages, levels of experience and ability. It has hardly ever been the case that a reader has not benefited from what I view as a mentoring or supervision session. I hasten to add that this is not because I know more than them but that with the experience I do have, I can offer an objective ear and voice that might just help.

PREPARATION

Given the above scenario, I have been ever surprised by the numbers of readers that experience difficulties and problems as a result of their work as a telephone psychic. This is apart from the common problems of awkward/drunk/silent callers, which we will deal with each in their turn. The issues to address first are those caused by lack of or incorrect/insufficient preparation and simply not adhering to the basics of psychic work.

When I first began in the role of managing or as I prefer, mentoring telephone psychics I was very surprised by the number that, despite being professional psychics, simply did not do the basics. They then wondered why they were continually drained, tired, depleted and/or ill. A timely reminder to them that these must be observed or such problems would occur usually did the trick – after I had reminded them what the basics are!

The value of mentoring or supervision for telephone psychics goes beyond a value for me, to a level of necessity. Given that you are working from home alone it is all too easy to become isolated, sloppy and unprofessional, the worst part being that you are unaware these deadly sloths have crept up on you. I will say more about this matter later in the book, but for now if you are able to accept the need for such sessions on faith or trust, we can make more progress together. As I say, I'll justify myself later!

Before any session or indeed just one psychic reading of any kind is given, by telephone or any means, certain preparations must be made and observed each and every time. There is no excuse for not doing them or sufficient reason for justifying to yourself you do not need to – ever. This is not just to ensure that you give of your best to your client, though this should of course be reason enough alone, but also to ensure both your and your clients' safety and well-being, psychically, emotionally, mentally and spiritually. If that doesn't convince you that you must follow something like what is given below, then probably nothing will!

One of the important psychic points to be made here is that most jobbing psychics do not deal with more than three or perhaps four clients in any one day and there is usually a healthy gap in time between each. This allows for safely and effectively releasing oneself of any psychic or energetic ties from one client before we open ourselves to another. The contrast with telephone psychic readings is that we can deal with easily twice as many people in one shift and they can follow at times thick and fast (this is not a slur on our beloved caller's character by the way!). This can present a danger of absorbing energies from a caller and being unable to release them before the next one is upon us and so we can have a cumulative effect over a few hours, leaving us clogged and blocked with all manner of energetic sludge by the time we finish.

To give a psychic reading of any kind requires of the reader that we are open at a psychic or at least intuitive level within ourselves and that we connect with our client or caller at this energetic level in order to give an effective reading of those energies. Regardless of your own individual awareness of this process, if you are working in any way psychically, it will happen. It therefore requires of us to open ourselves at the requisite psychic level before we connect with our first client on each shift, do our business, then close at that same level fully and completely before we continue with our own lives. As mentioned previously, failure to do so each and every time will inevitably result sooner or later in unwanted symptoms that if nothing else will mean you cannot work.

Whilst it can be an individual matter exactly how you prepare yourself, here is my recommendation. A good half hour before your shift you should have everything practical prepared and set up – your table ready, well-lit, water nearby, cards out and shuffled, your room comfortably heated or ventilated, the dog fed and walked and so on. Knowing that all this is done allows you to switch off mentally from such 'worldly' concerns so that you can give your attention fully to your work and your callers.

Next is a meditation or attunement process. It is not within the scope of this book to teach you how to do this and if you are totally unable to do this for yourself, then I would suggest that this is an indication you are not yet ready for telephone psychic work. Given that you are however, then my strong recommendation is that you first ground your self, by connecting yourself energetically with the Earth and allowing that natural flow of energy back up in to your body and being. Now open your higher energetic flow and allow a connection to the Universe, your Guides, angels, dragons, fairies, unicorns, aliens or what or whoever else you feel serves to achieve this. The point here somewhat sarcastically made (who me, never!) is that you need to achieve a strong and clear connection so that, like the Magician in the Tarot, there is a flow of energy that goes through and not from you.

Apart from ensuring that what you give your client is not your own thoughts or opinions which are totally irrelevant, this also serves to ensure that you will be sustained by this flow throughout your shift, and for as long as you need it to.

Continue to sit in this calm and quiet manner until you feel a balancing of these energies within you and a sense of peace and stillness comes to you. You are then what is said to be 'centred' and in the correct space to carry out your work. You may then like to say some words, silently or aloud, to ask your Guides to be present, to ask for protection and help in your work, offering yourself in service to your clients. A useful tip I have found effective is to ask to be connected only to those callers who it is right for you to speak with that day. This serves to help in reducing the number of crank, silent, drunk etc. calls that you will inevitably get.

You may have already lit some incense or essential oil to help lift and cleanse the energy in your room which is always helpful and preferable and now is the time to light a candle. This simple and easy ritual serves as indicator, for me at least, that I am connected and open and in a sacred space, so that everything I do is regarded as such as long as it remains lit.

Now you are ready to log on and are open for business! One last point before we look at the process of the call, is that to help reduce the possibility of 'psychic pollution' from the ongoing flow of callers, I recommend blowing out your candle at the end of each call, mentally sending the flame to that caller with your blessing. This ends your connection to them and can serve as a good energetic means of disconnecting the psychic connection between you. This can and will work, if you are clear in your intention that this is the case. I have used this process for many years and have passed it on to many readers, all of whom have found it to be effective.

INTRODUCTION

So, you have done your preparation, logged on and are ready and waiting for the 'phone to ring. Some readers find they have a case of 'first-night nerves' on their first shifts and of course it can take some time to get used to this kind of work, just as with any new job. This will soon settle down, be assured and rather than an immediate thought of 'oh my god' when the phone does ring you will soon find your thinking is 'Great, another reading' instead.

Every call can be a potential minefield however, as well as offering you the opportunity of changing someone's life for the better, forever. A professional and friendly start and introduction to every call will go a long way not only to diffusing any unexploded mines but also to set the reading up nicely both for you to give a great reading as well as the caller being able to get all they need from it.

Over the years I have extolled the virtues of the following beginning to calls to so many readers that it is a surprise to me I haven't given up out of sheer boredom of repetition! The main reason for the continuation is simple – it works!

The point can be well made here that many callers are distrustful of having a telephone psychic reading, however much they may want or need the help of a psychic. If we look at the scenario from the caller's point of view, they know it is a very expensive telephone call at £1.53 a minute (in sterling if you are outside these fabled isles), even though for a psychic reading it is not that pricey in reality – it is the psychology of the thinking. They have no idea who they are going to speak to (remember our psychic or psycho?), if it is genuine or they are going to get ripped of to the tune of £30 or more. Yet still they call. Such is clearly their genuine need.

So the beginning and introduction of every call is of prime importance, not just to that call, but to everyone that caller tells about their reading and you can be sure they will, good or bad; as the saying goes, you have only one chance to make a first impression and as we know, first impressions count. The friendly yet professional introduction to your calls should therefore be a pre-requisite, each and every time.

Not only does this set the call up effectively for you, it also serves to provide a continuing and recognisable standard that the Company for whom you work will thank you for. Without beating the customer repeatedly around the head with it, your standard introduction reinforces the corporate identity and subtly encourages the caller either to ring you again as their chosen psychic or to continue to use that company. Either way, it's a win-win situation for all. With all that in mind let me take your hand and walk you through the stages of the perfect introduction.

First is the manner and tone of voice with which you initially answer the call. A friendly and relaxed tone is required, as is a confident and welcoming approach that shows you are pleased to have received the call and are looking forward to helping your caller with a reading. Some readers begin rather with a vague and confusing 'Hello?', with an inference to it being a question. This serves only to confuse a potentially already apprehensive caller as they are hoping and waiting for someone to guide them through the process. If you start this way you are serving only to confirm an already underlying lack of faith or confidence in the caller.

So, when you have answered the call, stick a smile on your face, irrespective of how you feel, as this will automatically lift your voice, along with your energy a little too. Start with something like "Welcome to the psychic line" (your Company may want you to insert their particular brand name there, which is fair enough). Give them your name and your PIN number and tell them what you do. Giving your PIN number is first good business sense as well as simply polite and helpful. Many readers add to their PIN number the statement 'in case we get cut off'. This is not a good message to give out since it inherently implies that you might and there is no reason this should happen. Rather add here 'for when you want to get back to me'. Your attitude should really be that for each and every call you receive you are that callers psychic, any time they want or need a reading, so it makes sense to ensure they know who you are and how to get hold of you.

Then ask if you can take their name and immediately acknowledge this by saying "Thank you
 Fred". This gives them the message that you are listening to them and the fact that you have used their name registers in their awareness a little - a positive start. The first name is all that is required and some will refuse to give you their surname, which is understandable in these days of identity theft. It is also good to use their name through the reading at suitable intervals – without going over the top which just becomes artificial and annoying – apparently after we have heard someone use our name six times in a conversation our brains register more fully and deeply that we are being spoken to and we pay attention and focus more, which is surely what we as psychics want from our clients.

Then ask for their date of birth. The regulations require that on each and every call you must be heard to verify that the caller is over 18. This applies even if you run out of time on one call and they immediately ring you back. You can just ask if they are over 18, which is acceptable, but of course the answer will always be yes whether the caller is over 18 or not! By asking for a date of birth, should the caller be under 18 they will be forced either to have a fake birth date prepared or instantly make one up. If they do the latter, then it will be obvious and they will sound unsure and everyone knows their date of birth. If you are unsure whether they are over 18 going by the sound of their voice and their manner, you can then ask them to repeat their birth date, saying that you didn't quite catch it. If they have just made it up then they will not be able to and it will differ in some way.

Should you have doubt about their age then you are required to end the call. This is best done by simply explaining that you do not feel they are 18 and under the regulations you are going to end the call. Be polite and clear, thank them and hang up. You can of course give them your Company's 'Customer Service' number or equivalent, which all have, if they have any questions. The majority of under age calls are accompanied by giggling and questions such as 'whose gonna win the X-Factor' or 'what are the lottery numbers'? This gives you all the confirmation you need.

Next in the introduction we need to ask them if they have called us before or have used this service before. If they have not then you know you need to make a little effort to put them at their ease and explain things, which will always be welcomed. Tell them that while you are shuffling your cards or tuning into them psychically, you will let them know how it works.

Explain to them that they can ask any questions they like and you will focus on that for them or they can just tell you what area of their life they would like you to focus on of they prefer. Say that if they wish you can just do a general reading and see what comes out for them. However it is best to add to this that if they really do have a question or subject it is better to say so, rather than play a testing game to see if it comes up or not. It may well do but you may only have five minutes left of the call by then in which to deal with it. Say that with just 20 minutes to do the reading in, you want to be sure that you give them what they want. Given free reign, Spirit will give us the information they want us to know, which is not always what we would like to know!
This is not fishing for information, which is always to be avoided. This gives the impression you are a fake and need help. If you are a good psychic you will not need to fish for anything, you will know, so trust it and get on with it! If they sound at all nervous or worried explain to your caller that you will tell the, whatever information you receive for them but there is no need to worry as they will not hear that they will be run over by an errant no 42 bus when they are 60

years of age or meet an equally unlikely demise! Making a joke here will lighten the mood and set the caller at their ease. If need be, you can go further and explain that it is not the province of psychics to make negative predictions, readings are there to guide us and help us grow and any difficult situations are opportunities for growth and learning, with which your reading will help and guide them to the best possible outcome.

If they have called before, finding out how long ago this was can be useful. Firstly there should not be a need for a further reading soon after another. Sometimes people can be too keen not to make a move out the front door without having had a reading first, which is clearly not healthy. Secondly, there can be times and situations in which things can move and change swiftly and so another reading to re-assess a situation can be called for, which is perfectly acceptable. Finding out the background at this point is much better than taking half the reading just to uncover what has gone before, which if the caller already knows is pointless and they may just as well tell you now!

Sometimes callers can state that they have just had a reading with another reader but they would not tell them what they wanted to hear. Here of course there is the need to explain the role of readings is to give the truth as we receive it and that readings tell us the truth and that just like life, it is not always what we would wish for or like to hear, but it will help and guide us if we can allow it. Some will understand this and respond to it, others will not, but there is little else you are able to do in these cases. You can of course decline to read for them if you feel that a reading is of no use here but should this be the case be sure to tell them why, offering your reasons politely and patiently.

Now we need to find out why they have called. Some readers launch straight into a reading, just following their tried and tested formula. Listening to so many of these calls, after ten minutes of their wasted money or as soon as they are able to shovel a word in edgeways I hear the exasperated voice of the caller saying something like 'yes, that's all very well, but what I'm calling about is . . .' It is only then that the reading proper begins.

So it is well and advisable to ask the caller if they have a subject or question so that you can be sure they get what they want from their reading – be client led! Some 'clever' callers like to play what I call 'the psychic game'. This is where they either say (with the requisite superior tone) 'well, you're the psychic, you tell me'. At this stage I usually emit a small sigh and explain that I could easily give them a general reading but the chances are that they will hear some information about what their question or subject is but that they will also hear lots more besides. The result of this is that we will get about five minutes to deal with what they want, whereas if they tell me now we can get stuck in straight away and really help them. This usually does the trick.

Other callers pretend that they don't have a question but want to see if you will pick this up. This way they think they will be equally clever and test you without your knowing. The same as above applies here so really they have lost the psychic game before they have started! I tell these people that if there really is something it's best to let me know as it may come out or they may receive the information that 'Spirit' want them to know, which may well be different to what they want to know. Again, all we are really doing is trying to help you get what you need and give you a truly value for money service, dear caller!

Lastly in your introduction you may want to suggest that they grab a pen and paper in case they want to make any notes as you go. It is also good to tell them that readings are a two-way process, they are not about you talking at them, but rather you giving them information and them responding. Tell them that it is OK to ask questions, interrupt if they want and not to worry about putting you off. Give them permission to ask for more information or say if they don't understand or want further details on any aspect. This all helps to set them at their ease and lets them know they are involved and have an active role to play in the next 20 minutes or whatever, rather than being a passive observer. All this helps the quality of what is about to follow, which we shall look at shortly.

You may be thinking as you read all this that the twenty minutes will all be taken up with the introduction, since it's taken me three pages to cover everything that needs to be said. However, as the summary below will show you, it can all be done in just a couple of short minutes, two minutes that will show they are more than their worth in setting up the potential for a much more pleasant, worthwhile and generally successful reading for both caller and reader alike.

In summary then, the points you need to cover are -

- ⅄ *Welcome to the line, your name and pin*
- ⅄ *Callers name, date of birth/age verification, bill payer/permission*
- ⅄ *Your skills and type of reading required*
- ⅄ *Do's and don't during reading*

So your introduction will vary depending on whether your caller is a first-time caller or not. With this in mind, here are two typical introductions you may choose to follow -

FIRST TIME CALLER
Welcome to the psychic line, my name is Stuart and my pin number is 0930. Can I take your name please?
Hello (repeat name) . . . Can I ask your date of birth and if you are the bill payer on this line . . .
Have you used our service before?
OK, let me tell you how I work and then let me know what you want from your reading so I can
answer any questions you might have . . .
OK, I am just going to shuffle my cards/tune into you psychically so take a good breath and relax and we'll start your reading.

REPEAT CALLER
Welcome to the psychic line, my name is Stuart and my pin number is 0930. Can I take your name please?
Hello (repeat name) . . . Can I ask your date of birth and if you are the bill payer on this line . . .
Have you used our service before? . . .
OK, how long ago was your last call . . .
Do you have a different subject to look at today or any specific questions you'd like to ask?
OK, I am just going to shuffle my cards/tune into you psychically so take a good breath and relax and we'll start your reading.

So as you can see there are three pages worth of explanation behind this sleek, professional yet friendly beginning to your calls but it does not take long to deliver and get stuck into the reading, which is after all, what your caller has rung for.

One last thing to mention here before we begin to dissect the content of the calls themselves is that you need to pay attention to the tone of your voice. I have already mentioned that you need to sound relaxed and friendly but you also need to avoid sounding like a robot and that you are either reading a script or rushing through the boring bit. Some readers I have heard sound either like they are announcing the beginning of a TV programme or the departure of a train from platform 3, or rush through it so quick they could be commentating on the Olympic 100 metre final!

Neither of these approaches will help the fabric of the reading nor assist the caller in anyway. What is required is a tone of voice that demonstrates that you are relaxed, ready for the call and pleased that they have rung you. The best and most authentic way to achieve this is not to follow a script but in your first days have notes beside you of the points to cover and let the words come naturally to you. They will then be a little different for each call and you will not get bored or sound like a machine answering the 'phone – as I have heard some callers they thought say to their reader!

Now that we have all that nicely wrapped up, at long last let's take a look at the readings.

PRESENTATION AND DELIVERY

The manner in which you deliver your reading is perhaps of more importance with a telephone reading than it is face to face. You cannot see each others expression nor take advantage of the subtle but absorbed body language signals that we all unwittingly give off, as well as the more conscious gestures and mannerisms that we each naturally employ to add weight and expression to what we are saying and what we wish to convey.

This leaves us with just our tone of voice so it is vital that you are conscious of this and of how you come across and sound on the end of a telephone. A good suggestion here is to ask a friend to record you, or record yourself when you give a practice reading, which you really should do plenty of before you begin giving professional readings for a company.

Always be sure that you voice is positive, never raise your voice or sound distracted, be gentle when required in your delivery, empathic rather than sympathetic. Make your delivery a positive and empowering one, laced here and there with a touch of humour, where it is appropriate. The official line is that 'readings are for entertainment purposes only' (more of which later) and callers should actually enjoy having a reading and be something they would want to repeat – it is up to you to make this happen.

The above are just a random sample of some general guidance I have given to readers over the years, many of which could be classed as common sense perhaps, but a good number of readers can fail to achieve these things. We can all have an off day of course but the isolation factor of working from home and usually without any kind of supportive input, means that it can be all to easy for motivation to drop and we slip into bad habits, often unaware of the impact on our work and general standards. It is common for readers to react with surprise when I tell them some of the things they are doing and how they are sounding and coming across to callers. Either that or they acknowledge what has been said as the realisation kicks in of the habits they have got into.

Now let's look at some more specific issues regarding the presentation and delivery of your readings. An all too common fault can be when readers deliver their, often very good information, but as a question. The reader may say something along the lines of ' have you recently had a falling out with a friend or colleague and felt like they have been stabbed in the back'? Once the caller has confirmed this, the reader then goes on to give further information on this issue. However all this does is suggest to the caller that you have been fishing for information and used this to give your information. How much better it is to just come out with what you are picking up/seeing in your cards or whatever and just say 'I am seeing a falling out with someone around you here that's left you feeling like you've been stabbed in the back, can you understand that'? How much more receptive will the caller be when you then give further information and positive guidance, as you should, on how best to respond to the situation as it is now and make your predictions based on this for the final outcome of it.

The underlying premise here is to consider how confident you are in your abilities? If you are fully confident, as indeed you should be, there is no need to ask questions of a caller. As I have often said, dare to be wrong! You are a good psychic and will have been tested stringently to obtain your role, so your confidence is not misplaced. Make use of this and your readings and more importantly your callers will benefit all the more from it. So will you of course, as not only will you provide better quality and therefore longer calls, your caller will come back to you personally. This of course means that you will make more money and so your Company will love and value you all the more too!

Of course there are times that your caller, bless them, will not accept what you say. There can be many reasons for this, not just the fact that on this occasion, you re wrong. If you are, then so long as you know you have tried your best, done all your preparations and the introduction as you know you should, then simply admit it – this time you have not connected psychically with that caller. It may be because you are having an off day, or an off moment! It may be that guides have intervened for whatever reason and will not permit you to read for that person. It may be that you have been just too accurate and the caller is not able to let themselves admit what you have said as it is just too painful for them at that time. In reality the reason does not matter.

What matters is that you do not keep the caller on the line, dragging things along until they lose patience and trust in psychics and hang up with an exasperated huff! The best policy to adopt is one of 'three strikes and out'. If you have given three pieces of juicy information to your caller and they cannot or will not take any of them, it is best to politely and calmly explain that it is not their or your fault but you have been unable to make a connection with them psychically at this time and rather than keep them on the line suggest that they call back or better still refer them to your company's customer service number which they should have given you and they will find them another reader.

My experience has been that caller's respect this and do not display any annoyance, but are actually pleased with the honesty on display, which increases their faith and trust in the company they are using. This invariably leads to a much more successful reading for them when they call back.

The next thing on the 'things to consider' list is where it is inappropriate to give a reading. When we look at the regulations regarding premium rate telephone lines we will consider this further but for now let us be aware that should your caller demand any kind of health diagnosis, including that of pregnancy, you need to politely explain that the regulations do not permit you to do this and you must then be heard to recommend they see their GP or other registered health practitioner. It is acceptable to suggest ways in which the caller may help themselves with the aid of natural healing techniques, affirmations and the like if you genuinely know about these, but always cover yourself by making the point that this is not a substitute for a medical treatment.

This also applies should your caller say that they are being treated for depression or taking medication of any kind for a mental condition or be under treatment of any sort for this, such as seeing a psychiatrist or similar. The main reason for this, as you can explain to the caller, is that as a psychic you do not wish to contradict or work against the input from their counsellor/psychiatrist and create any kind of confusion for them.

Should you receive a suicidal caller, and this can and does happen, then you cannot deal with this. Many psychics are qualified counsellors and may indeed have the necessary training and skills to deal with those contemplating suicide. Even if this is the case however, you are currently working for a telephone psychic line, costing them £1.53 per minute and this is not the place to be dealing with suicide. These lines, officially speaking, are for entertainment purposes only, and this situation however you may look at it, is certainly not entertainment! What must be done in this case is to refer them to the Samaritans who are equipped and trained to deal with this. If your company does not supply you with it, and shame upon them if they do not, then have to hand the 'helpline' of the Samaritans in your area, which will be easily obtainable on the internet or local 'phone book.

Callers can ring telephone psychic lines for all kinds of reasons and sometimes because it is a viable alternative to dealing with the 'authorities' in whatever area their difficulty might lie. This may be an underlying alcoholism or other addiction, physical or other abuse – the only limits of drama are your imagination here. It cam be much easier and less confrontational for some people than facing something head-on, which contacting a specialist in their area of conflict can represent, to call a psychic line, asking for a general reading and hoping the situation is picked up and can then be gently admitted. Should this occur, all that you can do is to give the psychic information you get concerning it. Your own opinion is irrelevant, even if you have been in exactly that situation and think you know all about it. You can mention this, without going into detail, to empathise with them, but never give your view or thought. Give only the psychic information you receive and gently suggest that it would be a good idea if they were to contact a specialist that deals with people in their situation so they can get the help they need and deserve. It does no harm to have gathered the national help lines and/or website addresses of organisations dealing with alcoholism, drug addiction, battered women, crime victims, rape victims and so on. You may be unpleasantly surprised at what you might hear and be faced with, working as a telephone psychic - all of life with all its indiscretion, darkness and deception awaits you!

A footnote to this topic is that you must never, ever give out your personal telephone number to a caller, under any circumstances whatsoever, however heartfelt or tempting the situation may appear to be. If there is some kind of dire emergency, report the situation immediately to your company, as it is for them to deal with. I do know of one telephone psychic who 'lent' a four figure sum of money to a caller having made personal contact with them, for which they are of course, still waiting repayment. I also know of a caller who threatened suicide, genuinely as it turned out on this occasion, the attempt being thwarted when the psychic company contacted the police in their area, showing that this is the right action to take.

On a different aspect of telephone psychic readings, it is best to avoid saying that something, or indeed anything, will *definitely* happen. The majority of callers to telephone psychic lines, being usually ill-informed by an errant media who pander to the view that 'fortune-tellers' tell you what's going to happen and what your destiny is, there being nothing you can do to alter its course or change the outcome. The majority of psychics however, work under the premise that the future is not fixed and that part of the purpose of having a psychic reading and our ability to look into the future is to empower us – fore-warned is fore-armed, so to speak. Apart from being an entertainment, the ability to see our possible or probable futures is to help guide and inspire to create the future and outcomes that we want, rather than being the victims or playthings of fate. By giving any outcome or circumstance as a definite, however clearly you may see it in the cards, birth chart or hear your guides telling you, any one can change their direction, mind, heart at any given moment and so change the outcome of what you have seen. If you are telling a caller that anything is definite, this is ultimately dis-empowering to them and disrespectful of their right to choose, quite apart from going against the natural order of the working of the Universe.

It is better to give general guidelines in terms of time to callers, using whatever your particular method is in your readings. It is accepted here that astrologers can be more specific as they can pinpoint movements of planets into signs and houses to an exact date and even time, but again, how swiftly and in what way the caller responds to these influences and energies is for them and them only. Remember too here, that in the spirit world, from where our psychic information (arguably) comes, there is no time, this being a human invention for the sake of our organisation and applicable only on the earth plane of our existence.

That spirit world exists and operates at a faster and finer vibration that our own, even though it can be said to be all about us. Because of this, the information that we receive from our guides in the spirit world can come at a higher rate of vibration as well. This means that it comes very quick into our heads and out our mouths when we are giving a reading. So it is that some readers follow suit and their readings go at 100 miles an hour in a breathless whirl of wonder that leaves the caller not sure of anything that was said, by whom, when and how!

Communication with guides is a two-way process, so ask them to slow the delivery down a bit! Readers can sometimes think that a quick delivery is good for the caller because of the cost of the call. Of itself this can be a separate issue which we will deal with later in this chapter, but for now let's make the point that a large amount of information can be given during a telephone psychic reading and it can be quite hard for the caller to take all this in and remember it, the more so if it delivered at a speedy rate. Some callers may not be blessed with the highest IQ in their town, street or even house (is that a polite enough way of putting it?!) so keeping up not only with your knowledge but the information the spirit guide wants them to know can be all too demanding when it comes at them like a cartoon snowball rolling down a mountain – gathering size and pace every passing second! Like the cartoon, it all ends in disaster in a crumpled heap!

If you of the 'accelerated reader' tendency, a good practice to establish when giving a reading is to take a good breath after every sentence. Not only will this have the effect of injecting a structured pace to your reading, it also gives the humble caller a chance to take the information in and absorb it a little, even as most readers would hope, to jot down a note or two.

Excellent communications skills are of course a pre-requisite for any psychic worth their crystal ball and perhaps especially so in the case of telephone psychics. Be conscious of any accent you might have and do try to make your speech as clear as possible for the caller. A big part of communication is listening as well as talking. When I begin a telephone reading for a new caller, I always tell them that it is a two-way process and to ask any questions or say anything they wish as we go and not to worry about putting me off by butting in – if they want to, do so. Psychic readings are not about you talking at your client or caller, but you giving them the information you have for them and their responding to this. Using this tried and tested formula, you can then get to the heart or root of an issue for them and guide them to the best reading possible and way in which they can help themselves.

It is vital having said this of course that when they do speak, you listen! It is surprising how many times I hear a reader talk over a caller, which is simply wrong from so many aspects. Sometimes callers have a need to talk and can actually do more of the talking than you. I have done readings where I have indeed hardly managed to slide a sentence or two in, yet at the end of the call the caller has thanked me profusely, telling me who helpful I have been and how useful it was! Clearly their need was to offload, vent their feelings or just talk about their problems for a time. Having shifted this energy they then feel a whole lot better and will usually be able to view their situation much more clearly and objectively as a result, allowing them to respond to it in a more balanced and productive way, so yes, helpful I have been.

Part of the reason for this is practising the art of 'active listening'. This relatively simple yet effective technique is taught early on in the pantheon of counselling training and is one of which all psychics should avail themselves. This applies particularly to telephone psychic readings but is really an essential in any situation where we need to listen properly to what someone is saying.

The objective with the practice of active listening is to effectively meet our clients' needs. To do this we really need to hear what they are saying. This begins with our being non-judgemental and empathic. In any situation where you are dealing with the 'general public' and perhaps especially by telephone, there will be every extreme situation and viewpoint imaginable presented to you, and some beyond this yet despite this, we cannot judge and need to be able to offer an objective viewpoint that shows we understand their reality. Our own opinion is totally and completely irrelevant; that is not what they have called for and are paying to hear.

We should be clear hear about the difference between empathy and sympathy. Empathy is the ability to share another's emotions or sensations whereas sympathy has a tendency to convey pity and is ultimately dis-empowering rather than empowering, which should always be our objective as a psychic. Callers will sometimes ring a telephone psychic just because they are feeling low or fed-up in that moment and their need is to hear something positive and uplifting to give them hope. A show of sympathy is now what is required, making them focus more on their low spirit and feel sorry for themselves. A response such as 'oh yes, I can understand that feeling, I've been there' is so much better than 'oh you poor thing, I do feel sorry for you'. Chances are that they will not know you feel sorry for them as they would have hung up before you got that far!

Instead what is required from you is your enthusiasm and your attention. We need to demonstrate that we have heard and relate to what they are saying about how they are feeling or whatever statement they have made. This is best done using a technique called mirroring. This is simply where we sum up what the client has said, with something like 'so as I understand it, you are feeling low and fed-up as you've not heard from your boyfriend this week and are wondering if you did something wrong'. Sometimes using key words that the caller has used here can be a help in showing them we 'get it' and it is always good to focus on words they may have repeated.

By doing this you can both be clear about what you are dealing with and you can then focus on this in the reading. This also removes the need for you to ask questions, which any good psychic worth their crystal ball will not do. This technique shows the caller that you are human as well and they are not the only person to feel like they do, which it can often feel like when we are going through some kind of turmoil. It also sets up an open communication and very importantly tells the caller that you are on equal level to them, you are not sitting upon some throne in some lofty castle because as a specially evolved human being you have deemed to help them with your gift!

As the reading progresses do be mindful of the callers need to speak. You may give them the information that you see which could release a trigger in them and they need to offload and disperse the energy they have held on to around this. Let them speak as this is a vital part of the process. Psychic readings are a two-way process, they are not about you talking 'at' your caller. When they speak, let them finish, however tempting it might be to jump in as you can see what the response is in your cards or your guides are simply shouting at you what to say!

Do not rehearse what you are going to say while the caller is talking. Instead, just listen. You are a psychic and information on what to say will come to you when it is your turn! Do not try to be a mind reader, just be the psychic that you are. As has been said, what you think does not matter and you are not there to advise them on what to do. With the benefit of the psychic information that you give them, they can go away from the call more informed with information they did not have previously, feeling empowered and with choices at their disposal to decide what to do for the outcome they feel they really want.

This brings us to what callers want from their reading. Here we can run into some difficulties, caused mainly by the callers' expectations, media portrayal and readers stance. Many callers have the expectation that a psychic reading will tell them what is going to happen, with no perception or concept of freewill. Their pre-conceived reality, fed largely by an unknowledgeable media, is that this is what 'fortune-tellers' do; they predict the future. The idea that we may have some say in creating that future ourselves is largely foreign and so this can leave the reader somewhat perplexed when we are presented with the question 'is this definitely going to happen – I'm definitely going to meet him next week' and so on.

Here we can attempt to explain the nature of freewill, destiny and the scientific reality behind what is now trendily known as 'cosmic ordering', but at £1.53 per minute there are few people who wish to listen to our wordy explanations of the nature of existence and reality and just want to know if their man is definitely cheating or them or so and so from round the corner fancies them. All we can really do here is try and come up with a sentence or two that sums up the way things work and try to encourage our erstwhile caller to take a little responsibility for their own life and what they experience, or will do.

In this case, the ideal with psychic readings is not to make future predictions at all, but to be in the business of giving information using our psychic ability to our callers, that gives them additional information they would not have had access to otherwise. The aim should be, each and every time, to empower the caller and offer them choices and options as their next course of action that helps them achieve the outcome they desire.

The best means of achieving this in your psychic reading is to present the information you see as a story, a flow of information that moves easily from one card to the next or from one piece of information to the next. It can be easy to jump about from one subject to the next, especially when using the Tarot. This ends up confusing the caller as they try to fit the pieces of the jigsaw puzzle of a reading you have given them into one workable and understandable whole.

Many callers ask for a general reading and if this is the case, begin say with love and relationships and give them the information you have on this area of their life. Then move on to work and career, then home life and family, children if appropriate, interests and so on. By this time the 20 minutes of a premium rate call are highly likely to have run out anyway and your caller has received a coherent, well-structured and above all, useful reading.

It is also worth mentioning that there is a need to avoid talking about yourself too much in readings. Obviously this is not what the caller has rung to hear. It can be useful to demonstrate empathy, and we have seen how important this can be, but this can and need only be a sentence such as 'oh I understand what you mean, I once had the same experience and it left me feeling so sad for a time'. That's it, that's all that is required and the caller will hear the sincerity in your voice (it goes without saying that you should never claim to have experienced something if you have not). Try to avoid saying that you know how they feel – you do not. No matter how strongly you identify with them or think you know the feeling they might be describing, no two people are identical and they just might surprise you with their perception of an event. We all respond slightly differently.

A further point with presentation of your reading is that you should also never try to prolong your calls just to keep the caller on the 'phone. This is actually the quickest way to ensure they never call you back. Callers may be a little dumb at times, but they are not stupid and they sense and know when they are being taken advantage of. If you are a good and genuine psychic you will never need to do this anyway.

A useful tip or technique to have in your arsenal is to avoid asking the caller' do you have any questions'. I can guarantee that the answer will almost always be 'No'. This is because when you make this statement, what they hear you saying is that you have nothing else to say unless they want to ask anything. They know that they have called to hear the psychic information you have for them and if you have no more, then they will go. If you feel your information is drying up on a particular subject, then it is much better and more helpful for them to say something like 'ok, well before I move on to the next subject, what questions do you have on what I've said'. This keeps them involved, gives them the chance to speak and say anything they wish and lets them know you have more information to tell them. Many times they will of course, want to ask you questions.

Some callers are understandably reluctant to say much, if anything at all. This may be simply due to nerves or may be because they want to just listen to what you are saying. This can however, be quite difficult for us noble readers, trying to give of our best. Any relationship at any level, is never at its best when it is all one-way and that between psychic and client is no exception. This being the case it can be useful sometimes to tell them that you need to hear their voice occasionally to help you maintain the psychic link with them, which can indeed be the case.

Other than this, simply asking them, when you have finished a section of information or subject they have asked about, 'how does this make you feel' can be a good technique in encouraging them to open up a little, get some energy flowing and communicating with you or at the very least let you know they are still conscious! It is desirable to avoid asking anything that produces a yes or no answer. Instead opt for 'leading questions' as they are known, so-called because they 'lead-in' to an answer. Those beginning with 'who, what and why' and generally more effective than those beginning 'can'.

When delivering information psychically it is a good general rule of thumb to avoid seeing or presenting what you see or sense as a positive or negative. Again, the principle to work on here is   that life is rarely if ever, all good or all bad. If we look a little further there is nearly always some good to be found amongst the bad and of course, vice-versa. Instead, we should try to see life as a series of lessons for us to learn and so the need is to present our information so that our clients can see the chances and opportunities for them to grow and develop.

It is also of prime importance working as a telephone psychic that you are confident. This will show in your voice and if you lack faith, trust or ability in yourself, so will the caller. You may be the psychic one rather than them but they will still sense and know if you are not really convinced by what you are doing and saying and so neither will they. With a telephone reading the need is to engage the caller in the reading, perhaps more so than you would if giving a face to face reading. Communicating directly with them is the key to this, using their name frequently but not artificially, along with a combination of the other techniques presented in this Chapter. There is never any guarantee that every call you receive will result in a full-length, wonderful reading of impeccable quality but by applying the suggestions here you will not go far wrong and will at the very least know that you have given of your very best.

What remains then is to examine the regulations that govern premium rate telephone services, how to give a polite and professional conclusion and ending to your calls. Lastly we will then explore some more specific issues that some readers can find they have to deal with.

REGULATIONS

The regulatory body that governs all premium rate telephone services is called Phonepay Plus and exists to protect both users and companies and their workers alike. As such the regulations do not apply specifically just to psychic services, but all types of premium rate services, such as competitions, recorded services and adult.

Whilst we will limit ourselves here to an examination of what applies specifically to telephone psychic services, it should be borne in mind that these regulations apply 'across the board' as has been mentioned. The complete regulations are, in keeping with all things of this nature, lengthy and wordy, so I have here simplified what you need to know. You can and should however, view the full regulations at the following website -

The regulations state that service providers (this means both the company you work with and by extension, you) must use all 'reasonable endeavours' not to allow any talk or do anything that is likely to -

Encourage or incite a person to commit a criminal offence
Cause grave offence by reason of sexual or violent content
Involve the use of foul language
Debase, degrade or demean
Induce or promote racial disharmony
Encourage, incite or suggest to any person the use of harmful substances
Encourage or incite any person to engage in dangerous practices
Induce an unacceptable sense of fear or anxiety
Result in any unreasonable invasion of privacy
Mislead any person with respect to the content or cost of the service being offered
Prolong or delay the service unreasonably

If we look at these as a whole we can see that any decent psychic reading given with integrity will naturally not break any of these edicts. That said it can also be easy to be led, quote unwittingly or unwillingly, into breaking one or more of them by a caller, who themselves has no intention of doing so. Phone pay Plus can and do request recordings of calls at any given time and should it be heard that a call broke one of these regulations they, again can and do, issue hefty fines and at their worst can revoke a license to operate at all. This being the case it is as well to spend a brief time looking at the above list of commandments.

Whilst it may be simple common-sense that any psychic should not encourage anyone to do anything of a criminal nature, do bear in mind that you may well have callers from all over the world and different laws governing all kinds of things can exist in different cultures so if you are in any doubt whatsoever, always err on the side of caution.

There should be absolutely no question that a psychic reading should contain anything of a sexual or violent nature. However this is on the part of the reader but we cannot cover what the caller may come out with of course and in my experience they sometimes will make very direct sexual references! It is at this point that as the reader you need to be very careful and not engage with the caller in anyway and politely end the call. I do recall one reader who was the 'victim' of a man who was, shall we say, sexually indulging himself, on what was unfortunately her first shift. In her innocence and shock she said she would 'take a whip' to the caller, which even more unfortunately he liked the idea of! The call did however, soon come to an end!

Callers will almost certainly swear and use 'foul language'. Not all of them of course, but many people do swear as part of their routine and everyday speech. So, it must be said, do many readers. However, irrespective of however 'foul-mouthed' a caller may be, you cannot, ever, use any kind of swearing, however mild or inoffensive you may deem it to be. Of course, you should not be expected to have to endure being sworn at in anyway and you are perfectly within your rights to end a call if the caller is swearing at you.

This is quite different of course to a caller swearing as part of what they are saying and this comes down to what you find offensive and unacceptable. Should you do so, you can ask them once to not swear and use offensive language and then if they continue to end the call. Always, when you do end the call, be polite and clear, saying 'although I asked you to stop you are still using language which I find offensive so I am going to end the call. Thank-you for calling, goodbye'. Of course what you deem to be offensive may be different from the next reader and this is fine, we are each different. I would however, recommend the cultivation of 'rhino skin' in terms of your personal sensitivity if you are going to be a telephone psychic.

All the world and its curios await you at the end of the telephone, everything you could imagine will be presented to you and probably a few things you cannot, so it is as well to develop an open-minded attitude and unshakeable demeanour. This will result in your not falling foul in anyway of the next regulation to debase, degrade or demean any caller, which could happen by your simply reaction to something shocking a caller might say. As a telephone psychic you must always take a non-judgemental approach and attitude to your callers and this will ensure you do not fall foul here.

Next in our pantheon of do's and don'ts' comes discrimination. Again it really should go without saying (a silly statement since I am saying it here!) that you as reader can have no prejudice whether in terms of age, gender, race, religion, sexual identity or anything else I cannot think of that gets included in this list! Of course the same may not be true of our dear caller and they may and probably will display the most amazing prejudices. However unless they are being offensive, rather than simply stating their opinion, to which they are entitled, it is not for you judge or even react. It is far better not to bite and gloss over their opinion as such people often look for and delight in, a reaction and the shock value they think they can create with their oh so outlandish and rebellious views. Should you find it unacceptable and offensive you can of course decide to end the call, declining politely to continue.

This brings us to another point worth making here. As a self-employed 'contractor' you are entitled to choose not to offer your services to any person should you so choose. This means that you are within your rights to decline to read for anyone that comes your way and this is your prerogative. Of course it should be added here that you should at the very most be very selective in whom you decline. It is obvious that if you continually reject bookings or calls presented to you that you will not endear yourself to your company and in particular to the sales staff who may have toiled away selling your virtues and plaudits to a customer, only to find them back on the 'phone a few minutes later, wailing and gnashing their teeth having been rejected!

Callers come form all walks of life as we have said and in all shapes, sizes and indeed, states. This includes sad, happy, belligerent, argumentative, silent, and obsessed as well as it should be said, spiritually inclined, polite, receptive and appreciative. Callers will also be drunk and stoned on all manner of weird and wonderful substances and concoctions. Certainly some people will have a pint or glass of wine during the evening when they make their call and there is absolutely nothing wrong in this of course. However as the evening wears on and the drinks flow a little more freely, it can be great fun to ring a psychic for a laugh.

The degree of drunkenness or the caller is key to their suitability to be read for. A good company will use sales staff who can make an informed judgement call on this before they ever reach you, but those using the premium rate lines cannot be prevented. It is then that you must use your own judgement as to whether it is worth giving them a reading. It really comes down to whether they can receive the content of your reading coherently and sensibly and are able or capable of retaining it. If as the reading progresses it becomes clear this is not the case then it best to bring the reading to an end, perhaps in a light-hearted way, suggesting that they ring you back once the fog has clear and they are less lubricated! Most will accept this but should they insist on your continuing is is your choice whether to do so.

What should be made clear from the perspective of the regulations is that you cannot eve be heard to encourage them to use any kind of harmful substance. This really would include suggesting they pout themselves another drink while they listen to your utterances – you may not know if they are a struggling alcoholic and this suggestion is absolutely not in their best interests. The same goes for any drug use, of any kind. To be heard to do so would invite instant dismissal from any decent company and certainly risk a hefty fine.

The same applies here with regard to the caller placing themselves in any kind of danger, however slight, taking a risk with their behaviour or engaging in any sort of dangerous practice. If you are unsure you should always take a fall back position of safety and covering yourself by advising them to be sure what you have received guidance on for them is absolutely safe and they are not placing themselves in any kind of risk. What constitutes a dangerous practice can be different fro one person to the next but again, if unsure, do the sensible thing.

This leads us on to the next regulatory hurdle or pitfall if we see them that way, although we bear in mind they are there to protect the reader as much as the customer. This is regarding inducing or spreading any level of fear or anxiety in the caller. As a psychic who has the highest standards of ethics (as each and every psychic should) you will be concerned with this, but also with giving your callers the clear and absolute truth. This may mean you need to check or brush up on your methods of delivering your guidance and consider undertaking a course in communication skills.

Certainly no psychic should ever tell anything less than the truth, the whole truth and nothing but the truth, but how this is delivered is important. Rather than making negative predictions, we should strive to help the caller see them as challenges or even better opportunities for growth and learning – some readers refer to being tested but here I heartily disagree. The Universe has its way, not of testing us, but of creating what we project, for our own benefit and learning. How and why would it test us, it does not have emotion and does not care!

Anyway, I digress! It is important then to allay a callers fears or worries, and perhaps especially if they are a first-time caller. Some will be very worried about what they might be about to hear and I have had plenty say 'you won't tell me anything bad is going to happen will you'? I reassure them that I will not but that I will be honest and truthful and if there are some things that might be difficult for them, we will also look to see how they can best respond to and deal with it. This turns a worry into a positive and grabs their attention, in a good way!

For the Tarot readers amongst you there can be some pitfalls to be aware of where this regulation is concerned. In its wisdom, the Tarot includes all of life and as we know this is not always nice, fluffy, easy and wholesome, as some other more new-age based oracles would have you believe. As I tell my students, the Tarot tells it like it is. This can mean that you need to exercise caution where the regulations are concerned. It can be easy for the caller to jump into fear and anxiety as soon as you say something like 'your next card is Death and after that there's the Devil'. It is generally at this stage that they stop listening to you and instead lapse into some dark imaginings and horror of their own.

The advice I generally give to readers is simply not to mention card names at all, as a fail safe. You may well know that there are 'worse' cards in the deck – although no card should be seen as a 'good' or 'bad' card, they just are what they are and depict energies and it is how we respond to these that matter – it is what we do that makes our experience of them positive or otherwise. But for more on that, I refer you dear reader to my series of books on 'Tarot Therapy'.

By not mentioning any card names you cannot unwittingly cause worry or anxiety. Should the caller know a little about Tarot and ask what the cards are, you can of course tell them, but remember here that a little knowledge is a dangerous thing, so be careful with your responses and keep a positive and empowering stance

Now we come to any invasion of privacy. Whilst there are certain subjects that need to be avoided during a call, there can be some areas of a call that you may consider it unethical to enter into. Chief among these is when callers ask about a third party, wanting to know what they are thinking and feeling, usually about them! This is really a matter for your own conscience and I would suggest an equal number of readers do and don't consider this an invasion of privacy. For the sake of your business and ability to attract regular callers and making money I would certainly urge you to bear in mind that it is fair to say that the majority of callers do so for insight and guidance into their relationship in one way or another and this can will often include wanting to know what their partner feels about them, is thinking about, what's going on with them and so on. If you feel to delve into this psychically breaks your ethical code that's fine but be aware it will also limit your effectiveness and even usefulness as a telephone psychic in the eyes of many customers.

The penultimate item on our list of 'no-no's' deals with misleading a customer with regard to the cost of a call. The customer will have been played a recorded message before being connected with you telling them the cost of the call per minute and every advert must also include this information. This is not therefore something you need to overly concern yourself with, other than to ensure you are aware of the cost of a call for the customer, so as to given informed and accurate information should you be asked. It is wise then to know the cost per minute for the line you are on and what the cost is if they are on the line for say 10, 15 and 20 minutes.

Last on the list is the subject of prolonging or delaying the service, or any call, unreasonably. This is indeed an important issue for telephone psychics. To explain this, we should bear in mind that when psychic lines began they suffered, often justifiably from a bad press and reputation, such was the low standard of professionalism and quality. The customer has no idea who they will speak to when they call, if they are genuine or simply someone who will just tell them what they think they want to hear, which no psychic should ever do.

Many customers will now know that you will be paid per minute for each call that you do and for your part you must ensure that you are not motivated by the idea that the longer your calls last, the more you will get paid. Whilst this is true, any good psychic should struggle to get all they have to say in a 20 minute call and in this way, good durations take care of themselves. There should never be any need to even think about keeping a caller on the line for longer. The flow of information should easily fill 20 minutes, so long as the caller is happy to stay on line with you.

Perhaps because callers already have their guard against being ripped off, they will easily and swiftly sense and know if you are just trying to prolong a call for the sake of it and they will hang up. Should they decide to lodge a complaint with Phone pay Plus the recording of your call will soon reveal if this is the case and a fine or worse could easily result. In summary then, if you feel a need to even consider this or find yourself thinking along these lines, then you need to review your position as a telephone psychic. It is not only unethical but also suggests you are lacking the required confidence or even ability necessary to do this work.

READER ISSUES

This brings us nicely to issues that we can face as readers, just to balance things out a little! Aside from the ethical and other matters covered above, there can also be certain dilemmas the reader can face to ensure they are giving the best service they can and that the caller gets what they require.

In my experience chief amongst these is that of the cost of the call. Obviously the reader has no cost (not material anyway!) but he cost to the caller can be considerable and some noble readers genuinely worry about this on their behalf. Perhaps the reason for this is that the majority of readers would charge a fair bit less for a one to one reading than the equivalent cost by 'phone.

As the current rate of £1.53 per minute the cost of just a 20 minute reading by 'phone exceeds £30. Most readers do not charge much more than this for a reading lasting an hour, or indeed however long it takes; many prefer to not set a time limit, Should the reader have this to the forefront of their mind when they receive a call, this can create a number of issues, all of which ultimately detract from the callers experience. Before we explore these issues, it is worth saying that the bottom line here is that it is the caller's choice to call and we should respect that and their requirement of us giving our best to them. They are of course in control of how long they stay on the 'phone for and rest assured, they will be fully aware of the cost they are incurring and will moist certainly end the call if they do not wish to prolong it.

One of the ways over-concern about the cost of the call a reader may have can manifest, is that of speaking too quickly. Some readers speak so quickly as to become almost incoherent in their rush. This has the effect of confusing the listener and the human brain cannot retain information delivered at the speed of light! This type of delivery is disrespectful of the caller and does not give them chance to absorb and process what you are telling them. As you move perhaps from subject to subject in your reading the caller is left bemused and bereft as to what they have been told.

As we have seen earlier in this Chapter, information received from the higher vibratory levels of the spirit world can come to us swiftly, because of that faster moving vibration. It is your job as a reader to translate this in a form understandable and acceptable to a client and this includes slowing it down. If you work consciously with your guides (or even if you don't) ask them to slow it down! Another method of achieving what the caller requires in terms of speed of delivery is simply to take a breath at the end of each sentence. This allows the caller a chance to do the same and for what you have just said, to work its way a little into their receptive grey matter.

We should also perhaps mention here that concern about the cost of the call means that as a reader, you know you are not giving of your best and this will ultimately create a dissatisfaction in you. The vast majority of readers are very honourable fold with high degrees of ethics and this dissatisfaction will bother them. Therefore head it off at the pass and take your time! If you are relaxed in your approach you will not come across as rushed, which if your delivery is as quick as quick can be, the caller will hear and assume you wish to get rid of them as soon as you possibly can.

On another level, rapid delivery will mean your calls do not last long, which your Company will not like and your earnings will be reduced. Premium rate telephone calls are now an accepted part of our society, for good or ill, and following some recent and ultimately welcome scandal from television shows, abusing the service, they are more strictly regulated than before. This means that people are used to a telephone call costing them £1.53 a minute, whether they are voting for their next pop superstar or dancing celebrity, an adult service or having a psychic reading. So avoid the psychological trap of thinking it is costing them a huge amount, they know exactly what the cost is and choose to speak to you.

Consider what your worrying about the cost of the call says about your self worth too. Do you believe that the service you give is not worth £30 or so? If so, why and what do you need to do to address this and correct it? If we have worries about the value of what we are doing, we need to look and see what the cause of this is. What you are on the inside will be reflected on the outside. Value yourself and the caller will value you and the service you provide for them.

Lastly here, ask yourself if you really can give a good quality psychic reading commensurate with your skills, knowledge and experience in 10 minutes? A reminder here too that callers are told twice before they speak with you of the cost of the call, once in the advertisement and once when they make the 'phone call.

TELL IT LIKE IT IS

When people ring for a telephone psychic reading it is because they have a need. What that need is can be wide and varied. It is the job of the psychic at the end of the telephone to tell the caller the truth.

This is whether it will be what the caller would want to hear or not.

Of course how we do this is of paramount importance, but the point must be stressed that the truth must always be told by the reader; indeed the truth, the whole truth and nothing but the truth! This needs to be done with sensitivity but blended with directness. It can be tempting to always tell the caller what they would like to hear and if you are tempted by this particular sin, I would recommend you consider whether to do so would ultimately be of benefit to the caller. True it may in the short term help your averages engaging them in a call for longer this way, but rather stick to your highest integrity and tell them what it is you actually really see.

It may be true to say that the vast majority of responses to the question of 'is my boyfriend coming back' and 'does he really love me or not' are 'no' but if you are able to deliver this is a gentle, understanding and sympathetic manner, then you are more likely to be able to progress in your reading for this poor unfortunate to an exploration of how they can best respond to this malady that afflicts them and offer some guidance as to how they might avoid a repetition of the same thing in the future, as tends to be the case if we do not learn as we go. Those callers that are open to this are the ones that can really benefit from a reading at this time. Others will undoubtedly hang up on you without so much as a 'by your leave' as soon as you tentatively hint that their long lost first love of 15 years ago may not be getting in touch next week. However I personally would rather this than lower my standards of honour and integrity by not telling the truth as I receive it, however unwelcome and hard this may be for them.

Of course this does not apply only to relationship situations and the domain of the broken-hearted. There are many and varied causes that callers will present and always they deserve and should receive the truth. It is the manner of your delivery as a reader that requires the most attention here. I have known readers that have admitted that they tell the client what they would like to hear, which should be avoided at all costs. It is clear that often the reason for this is a fear of how the caller might respond. Should you know in your heart that this is the case with you, then I exhort you to undergo some basic counselling training (which arguably should be required by law for every professional psychic) and this will equip you with the necessary skills and techniques to respond in an appropriate, respectful and helpful manner to your caller.

Much as the importance of the truth cannot be over-estimated we should also say here that the presentation of cold, bare facts can hurt and be hard to hear, no matter how sensitively we feel, think or hope we are putting it across. We should always therefore, back up our 'yes' or 'no' answer with as explanation which should always be the reason behind our answer. We must then be prepared to respond to and answer any and all questions the caller may have, no matter how ridiculous or superfluous they may appear to be to us. To the caller that is their reality and we are there to help and serve them. We should always display the utmost patience and be equally prepared to answer the same question put in a different way as many times as is necessary for the caller to accept it. Indeed we may need to repeat ourselves, sometimes over and over, in our responses as the caller goes through the understandable mental procedure of assimilating and acceptance of the information they have been given. They may then need reassurance and repetition in order to do so.

CONCLUSION TO CALLS

We have previously covered the importance of the beginning, introduction and presentation of each and every call and now we must place the same importance to the ending of our calls If we are to maintain the same professional standards to our work as we would like ourselves to be given, then bringing a call to a friendly and professional conclusion should be the norm, as opposed to a simple 'thanks then, 'bye' approach or simply keeping talking until the call is cut off at the end of its allotted time, which is worse.

The majority of lines in business now have what is commonly called a 'whisper message' that will alert you that you are approaching the end of your call time. This is a recording that most impolitely but usefully butts in and tells you that you have, usually 2, minutes left to conclude your call. Both you and the customer hear this.

When this does play, you need to stop speaking. Many readers try and talk over it and all this does is create confusion as nobody can hear two voices speaking clearly at the same time. When the recording finishes there is always hesitation and doubt in the caller, so when you hear the message, stop talking, let it play and then you both know you have two minutes left.

It is up to you at this point to take control of the process as the caller will not usually know what they should do or say now. The whisper message is there for your use, so use it! What you say will depend on the nature and stage of the call, but here are some basic guidelines to help you. What is most important at this stage is that you remain calm and confident in your tone and approach and this way the caller will respond in turn and you will avoid the rushed approach that can happen and ends things messily and unprofessionally. Two minutes is much longer than it may sound and is plenty of time to say what is necessary and conclude things as both you and the caller would like.

Obviously the first thing to do is to finish the sentence you were in the middle of when your whisper message barged unceremoniously in! As said, what comes next depends on where you are at in the reading, which can vary a great deal.

If you have plenty more information to give your caller and clearly it would have continued naturally for some time longer, then it is best to tell them. Let them know that the call will be cut-off shortly but you have plenty of information still to come and invite them to call you back. You will then need to give them any instructions necessary for the process your particular line employs to do so. There is nothing wrong with this invitation – given that you do have information to give them you are simply trying to complete your work to best effect. It is their choice whether they call back or not of course. So long as your motivation here is not to get more money out of the call, it's fine.

Should you know however that you have very little information still to come when the whisper message plays, then it is really for you to take the lead and bring the call to an appropriate, professional conclusion. Either way, it is for you as reader to always take the lead here and you can be sure the caller will then follow.

You should complete the sentence you were on before you were so rudely interrupted and then just explain that as the call will end soon you need to wind things up. It can be very useful for the caller if you now give them a brief summary of the content of the call, briefly re-iterating the salient and most important points you feel they need to take note of.

Should the caller interrupt or say at any point that they want to ask just one more thing or have another question, it is best at this stage to tell them that you do not really have time to do this as the call is about to cut-off and you prefer to give proper answers rather than anything rushed or hurried and not as accurate as you might wish because of this. Again, this is not a sales pitch but a means of ensuring you stick to your highest principles and professional approach to your work.

Once the information in the reading has come to a conclusion by whatever means you then need to give a brief, friendly and yes, professional reading. I make no apology for the overuse of that word and will doubtless do so many more times before we are done, but I do feel that since the dawn of this new age of telephone psychic work the professionalism that could be said to have been lacking in our chosen work has been diagnosed with an almost terminal condition so I am merely doing all I can to bring about a resuscitation if you will forgive the rather ill thought out analogy!

Back to our conclusion. This should start with thanking the caller for ringing and speaking with you. Next remind them of your name and your PIN number for when they want to speak with you again. It also does no harm here to tell them your regular hours of work, if you have them. Wish them well and say goodbye.

As with all aspects of giving a telephone psychic reading, confidence, friendliness and above all professionalism (told you!) are primary to a helpful, positive and satisfactory conclusion to your call. As with the introduction this will soon become habit and second nature. It is at this stage that you must work each and every time to ensure that your voice does not carry an automatic tone, as if it is churning out the same thing every time, even if you are! This will come across as sounding insincere and false which could undermine all trust and belief the caller has built up at what you have told them over the course of your call.

BETWEEN CALLS

After the call has finished it is unlikely (and preferable) that you will get another call straight away. This is time you need to use to best effect. First you need to ensure you disconnect psychically and energetically from your caller. If you have lit a candle at the start of the call this should of course be extinguished now. Mentally wish them well and send them the candle flame. This little ritual comes highly recommended and is simple yet effective.

It is good them to record details of the call, either simply on a sheet of paper or more commonly on your pc's spreadsheet programme. This should have the time of the call, any call identification used by your service, the callers name and date of birth and the duration of the call. From this you can also calculate the amount you have earned from the call and so therefore a running total for the week, month or whatever pay period is used.

Now is your chance to visit the toilet, stopping en route to put the kettle on as you go, reaching for the biscuits on your way back! This may not sound as daft as it perhaps should since it is known that psychic work can have the effect of reducing blood sugar levels. Maintaining a good and healthy level of this can then be important to ensuring you are always able to give of your best to every caller you get.

After the necessaries have been addressed, it then become a matter of occupying yourself until the next call comes to you, which could be any any given moment of course but equally could be some time. Given that you are unlikely to simply sit there, whatever you choose to do should be something that helps you keep your energetic vibration raised while you are still 'on duty' so to speak.

You could most certainly have a meditation or relaxation practice, so long as you do not go too deeply into this and so either not be focussed or alert when the telephone rings or miss the call completely. A light visualisation style meditation or simply relaxation breathing exercises are perhaps best.

An excellent practice for between calls is reading. This keeps you mentally alert yet relaxed. The subject matter should be taken note of however, since the latest horror novel is unlikely to be conducive to a raised energetic vibration. Rather keep your material to spiritual, enhancing and positive subjects. It is a great time to feed your mind with healthful information. Further to this there are a good number of psychic development and spiritually related courses that can be taken online or by distance-learning and you could also consider these to keep you occupied between calls, whilst giving you some ongoing professional development (tax deductible, more of which later!) for your pains. Lastly, you could even write a book, which the fact you are reading this is proof that this can work!

END OF SHIFT PROCESS

Let us now fast forward to the end of your shift. You have completed your last call, blown out your last candle and completed your records. What comes next?

First, log off your company's system. This will either be a simple click or two on their website or a quick telephone call. Whatever it is, don't forget. You can be particularly sure that if you do, the telephone will ring from someone expecting a reading and you can be even more sure that this will be when you are asleep!

Next comes your own grounding and detachment, creating a return to your 'normal' (an unusual concept for psychics in my experience), everyday self. This should first consist of a meditative or energetic process that clears the vibration of your callers from your energy field and then grounds your own energies. There are many and varied methods of doing this effectively and if you are a practising professional psychic then you should know how to do this.

Again, do not neglect this. It can be so easy not to bother when you are tired or think to yourself that it doesn't really matter, nothing will happen. It does matter and something may very well happen. This will be a gradual yet subtle deterioration in your own energetic vibration that will slowly drag you down with it. I have seen this happen a number of times and the end result if left is always the same. This is that the reader becomes too tired to work and usually ill to force them to stop so their energies can recover and regenerate. When I come across a reader suffering this way and ask them what they do at the end of their shift, the answer is always the same: nothing.

So do take the brief time and care required here to make this a habit. If your shift has been a particularly draining or demanding one you like to generate a good healthy flow of orange light into your auric field to give you a boost - although not if you are shortly going to bed! Lastly part of your process here should be to give your thanks for those unseen beings that will have helped and guided you in your work. This should be done irrespective of your awareness of them or your particular individual beliefs – spirit guides, angels, ancestors, fairies, dragons, imps, elves or whatever should all be given due credit!

Now clear away any and all equipment you use for your work. This process should be part of your closing ritual and tells your own mind you are switching off and your work is done. This will help you relax all the more when you wish to. Now, even if you are longing to collapse into bed consider having something to drink and a snack, as your system may well thank you for it when it is relaxed. It can also be good to do something everyday or worldly, even if just for a short time. This is just to cement your return away from that inner world we psychics inhabit much of the time and implement a total and full return to the outer, everyday conscious level the rest of you live in!

So, that's what you do and how you do it! Now we will have a little look at our erstwhile customer, without whom of course, we would not be here.

CHAPTER 3 – THE CUSTOMER

We come now to the lifeblood of the telephone psychic world – the customers. These of course come in all shapes and sizes and with as many questions, subjects, attitudes and approaches as you might perhaps expect and some you may not! As we examine these here can I encourage you to keep an open and non-judgemental mind, as this you will surely need in dealing with all that will undoubtedly be thrown at you.

It should be made clear from the outset here that the majority of callers to telephone psychic lines are good and genuine people with equal needs and questions they want guidance on and answers to. That said of course there are exceptions to every rule and perhaps especially so in the telephone psychic world, such is its nature.

The psychic world by its very nature has always had a tendency to attract those who do not take the normal or accepted approach to the world and its workings and can go further than this in pulling toward it those who choose to exist on the fringes of what is seen as accepted and normal. If you are a practising psychic already it will not be hard for you to accept it when I say that we psychics can also have a tendency, and indeed are sometimes required to, see things from a different perspective, such is our nature and business. Indeed it is precisely this that a great many callers that we speak to want from us.

Many people consult psychics, whether in person or by telephone because conventional routes, support networks and systems have, for whatever reason, failed to give them the answers they need and so they look to an alternative, which is where we come in.

Being mindful of this, it is our job to give them the guidance and answers that we see for them using our chosen or given psychic tool or ability. It is a necessity to always be honest in this, no matter what your opinion or even judgement may be of their course of action. Customers can and will, challenge our values and moral choices and, beyond common decency and the law, it is not for us to question why and certainly not for us to judge or even give our own opinion; that is not what they call to hear and as I have stated previously, our own opinion is irrelevant.

We should of course report to the company we are working with anything unlawful or if you are concerned that a caller may be likely to cause harm to themselves or another and here our responsibility starts and ends. Even if you a qualified counsellor, therapist or general miracle worker in any other chosen field, this is a telephone psychic line and this is why you are here. If you perceive that a caller is really in need of counselling, therapy or any other professional intervention or help, then you should suggest this to them, sympathetically and positively, pass on a contact telephone number and leave it at that.

What should always be borne in mind as you conduct your work as a telephone psychic is that the person you are talking to is not just a disembodied voice on the end of the telephone but a real person, with a real life and an issue or issues that they need help with. If you are not bothered or genuinely concerned for them and whatever their dilemma may be, then you should not be there. What you say to them may have real and dramatic consequences, not just in their lives but any number of other people who may come to be affected by the choices and decisions your customer makes. So there is a big responsibility that comes with psychic work and you must be aware of this in each and every moment of each and every reading that you give.

Your responsibility is to fulfil this during your reading and then to let it go. Psychic work is in this respect a work of service, regardless of how much we do or do not earn from it. Once you have fulfilled that, you can relax, knowing that you did the very best for your customer and after that, it's up to them.

CUSTOMER ATTITUDES

Telephone psychic readings differ from those we might give face to face in that those who choose to come and see us have sought us out for a specific purpose or for a particular need. They bother to book beforehand, make a journey to see us and keep to an appointed time-slot. This all indicates that they are motivated strongly and that they have a belief or at least a hope or knowledge that the services of a psychic are right for them and that they have a belief structure that accepts what we do.

This can be very different to chancing upon an advertisement at the back of a newspaper or magazine, endorsed by some celebrity or other who promises all manner if minor miracles (in a maximum of 20 minutes!) if we call the number below. It can be, perhaps all too easy for someone to see the advert then pick up the 'phone with an attitude of 'I'll give it a go, you never know'. This is very different to the client who has sought us out and presents with a specific, identified need.

Callers can then sometimes have an attitude of 'you're the psychic, you tell me' when they call. This is a typical response we can hear when we ask them why they have called and what they would like a reading about and is, of course, entirely unhelpful. What is required on our part then (having taken an inward and silent 'big sigh') is to patiently and politely explain that we only have so long to complete their reading in and so if they have a subject or area of life they would like to focus on, it helps for us to know so we don't waste time looking at other things. This is usually enough for them to tell us why they have called or if not, we can elicit the truth that they just saw an advert and rang out of curiosity and/or the hope of hearing something good. This being the case we can proceed with giving them what is known as a 'general reading'.

This can then reveal that they rang hoping to be told what they wanted to hear, whether this was that they would get the job they have applied for or always wanted, or that they would meet and marry the man of their dreams and so no – in short thee really only wanted to hear what they wanted to heat and nothing else. I have heard so many readings over the years where the caller responds to what the reader tells them with yes after yes but their tone indicates that they are not really happy. This is clearly because they are not hearing what they hoped or longed to, but readings, just like life, rarely do this. Our business is the truth and this is not always or even often, what we want to hear.

On a deeper level this attitude can show that this caller has given their power away to a level that they just have faint, distant and unrealistic hope that something or someone will come along and grant their wishes. Not many of us are lucky to even find a lamp, let alone one with a resident genie, ready to grant our every wish! Here the reader may be able to work with the caller a little to help them to see the need to take back control over their self and life and set about the business of creating what they want and need.

Sometimes however, it is all we can do to explain to them that as a psychic we are not here to tell them what they would like to hear but to tell them the truth as we are shown it and this is not always easy or what we would like.

This attitude of giving away one's power is quite common and can also be shown by the caller who simply refuses to say anything for fear of giving us any information that we would use to dupe them. This can demonstrate a basic level of mistrust – not in us as a reader or psychism generally, but rather in themselves. That they do not want to tell us anything shows that they want proof first we are genuine and can tell them things we could not possibly know otherwise.

When presented with this attitude I take the approach that they are welcome to tell me as much or as little as they wish but again, there is a time limit and I can help them much more if they can tell me what subject they want me to look at so I don't waste half the time talking about other areas I might see before we get to what they really want. One word will do, 'work' 'relationship' etc. but if I have just this it indicates some willingness and openness to what they may be told and guided to do. This at the very least tells me I have chance of being heard.

The other way a similar attitude can be displayed is by those who say very little by way of feedback through the reading. These people have a tendency to grunt or make other indistinguishable, animal-like noises in our pauses between information. This indicates neither approval nor disapproval so we have nothing to 'feed-on' from their perspective. Again this can show a lack of faith, trust or belief in the reader which is really just a reflection of the same in themselves.

Giving a psychic reading is rather like a musical or any other creative performance done before a 'live' audience (there wouldn't be much point doing it before a dead one!). The artist performs their selected repertoire and the audience responds. The artist feels this warmth and feeds off the energy and this stirs, motivates and propels them to perform better and give just a little more. This lifts the crowd further, more energy flows and on we go until it all ends in rapture. This is why football teams often describe their noisy support as being like an extra man. So it is with a psychic reading. Even if all we hear is the word Yes or No, we then know that you are being listened to and that there is a flow of energy that is at least in some ways being responded to. This energetic flow is the currency that we use to do our work. Grunting just doesn't cut it!

So when presented with a grunter we may need to explain, probably in more simple terms, the above need for something appropriating a human response as we go through the reading. This will usually be met with an 'ok' and will require a few promptings from us before the penny drops and it clicks that they do need to speak now and again – this being the essence of any good telephone conversation! As we have seen this approach is often there to mask the desire to hear what they want to hear. Perhaps to state the obvious though, we are not there as a psychic to do this, but we are there to tell them the truth as we are given or perceive it.

Other customers can take an attitude of disagreeing with pretty much everything we say or give to them and taking a contrary view in general. These people tend, when we have told them something that they cannot disagree with, respond with a 'yes, but', usually swiftly by their justification for why this would be highly likely or anyone with an ounce of common-sense would say that. With these lovely folk we can but persist and try again to present the information we receive to them, in the hope they will acquiesce and open up to us. If however, we cannot break through their castle-like defences, then a good ploy is to state calmly and politely, using their name first, that they have asked us for a psychic reading which we are trying to do, but that they have chosen disagree or take issue with, or at the very least not accepted everything that we have said. I will then either ask them why this is so (which will usually get the reply that none of it is true) or what it is they want me to tell them or hear or what they would like me to focus on. This tends to   have the effect either of bringing the call to a conclusion or getting them to acknowledge the error of their ways and then opening up. Either of these is preferable to continuing to drown ourselves in a sea of indifference, mistrust or even ridicule.

As a telephone psychic we do need to be aware of the tendencies our customers will present us with and there is a need to develop something of a 'rhino-skin' to do this work (i.e. thick and impenetrable). We will occasionally get two or more people who think it the most hilarious thing to call a psychic and giggle hysterically at each thing said. If this is done in the right spirit there is nothing wrong with it at all and indeed can be great fun for the reader too, so long as we are confident in ourselves and not too sensitive personally.

Callers will have no compunction in hanging up without even saying a word to us, while we are busy working away on their behalf, with no warning and no clue as to why. We can be left wondering what we said, Tarot card forlornly in hand about to bring them a wonderful piece of news but left bereft and alone with only the buzz of the disconnected 'phone line for company! There can be several reasons why these callers hang up. It can be they did not hear what they wanted as we have already seen or they did not like what they heard (not the fault of the reader – don't shoot the messenger!), or, as is quite common, their partner walks in and so they cannot now talk about the affair they have been having and so on. Whatever the reason may be, as the suffering psychic at the other end, we can do nothing, but check to see if we have sprung a leak in our rhino-skin and if so patch it up, then go about our business. Certainly is it good to take a look and consider if we said or did anything wrong, or could have put anything differently so we can learn from the experience. In doing this, follow what your conscience tells you and you will not go wrong. Once this is done, forget it and move on to the next person.

Other customers will take great delight in telling us aggressively how terrible we are (though they will be guaranteed to use rather different terminology) the first time we say something that is not absolutely and specifically, irrefutably true. This can then be followed by a request to perform impossible physical tasks before hanging up, with as much force and gusto as can be managed. These angry people can be very hard to break through to, so the best thing here is to simply let go, forget it and move on, rhino skin intact.

All this notwithstanding, it should be said here that the majority of callers display a welcoming and warm, receptive attitude, are polite, agreeable and appreciative and can even develop into what we could call friends, even though you never meet. I have simply pointed out here the not so nice exceptions that exist in every area of life to help prepare and protect you.

So it is we see that customers present not only many different approaches, attitudes and therefore challenges for us to learn from, but also a wealth of situations and problems, just as life tends to do to all of us. Let us have a look now at some of these and see how we can best respond to these sometimes astonishing, perplexing and sometimes plain weird and wonderful questions.

TYPICAL QUESTIONS

Perhaps predictably and understandably, the majority of readings you will give as a telephone psychic will concern relationships, in all their many and varied incarnations, twists and turns. Whilst this may tell you much about the nature of us as people, it should be borne in mind that most people turn to a psychic to help them because something is wrong and they need help.

So we can work pretty much on the assumption that where we are dealing with a relationship issue, all is not as it should be for the caller. Very many times you will find that the caller's relationship has come to an end and they are calling to see if they will be re-united and if their boyfriend will realise what he is missing and come back to them. Clearly the caller is hurting and perhaps looking for some reassurance that all will be well and they can avoid having to face the pain and hurt of the end of a relationship and often, the guilt they are feeling from some action they now regret.

A sensitive and empathic approach is clearly required here but we should also be clear that although we may feel sorry for them, this approach will not help – we need to be empathic, not sympathetic. As a sensitive reader yourself, for this goes with the territory, you may well be tempted to tell them that the boyfriend they so publicly betrayed and ridiculed will forgive them and return to their outstretched arms and declare undying love and marriage, the reality is that the vast majority of the time, the relationship has come to an end for a good reason and is unlikely to be re-kindled. Of course there is an exception to every rule such as this, but in my experience it really is the exception.

It is also true to say that some callers are too rigid, fearful or plain blood-minded that they only want to hear what they want to hear. With these good souls there is little we can do, we cannot help someone if they are not ready or do not wish to be helped. Usually they will not even give us the chance, for as soon as we suggest that their husband does appear to have settled down with his new love and the child they have just had and that the divorce did speak plainly, they will hang up, usually with you in mid-sentence, just about to suggest the possibility of someone new entering their life! Let them go, do not react and send them blessings and love in hope of a little light finding its way into their regretful heart. Then move on to the next caller.

We should make it clear here that it is always and entirely the right thing to do to stick to the truth, as I have said elsewhere in this little tome. It does not help to tell a caller their boyfriend is coming back despite his new career, move overseas and new wife! You may think these light-hearted examples and far-fetched but I promise you not so. I have personally given and heard many, ,any readings of this kind. In one I just could not see any kind of connection or even link between the caller and the object of her affections, who she insisted was right for her. Having tried to get this across I eventually asked her how long it was since they had had any kind of contact. Following her response I gently tried to explain that after three years it was perhaps unlikely they were destined to be together forever! So always remember that your duty as a psychic is to tell the truth. Do this sensitively and gently where required, but always do it, even if it is pretty much a certainty that the caller will hang up on you.

I have mentioned a little earlier the importance of developing a 'rhino-skin' to avoid opening yourself to being hurt when callers do hang up and retaliate in inappropriate ways. Similarly you will need to develop a guard against judging others morally in terms of their behaviour. Equal to the frequency of 'is my boyfriend coming back' is the question 'will he leave his wife'. The first few months in your career as a telephone psychic will soon demonstrate the frequency of the 'eternal triangle' and will show you that it usually ends in tears. Yours however, is not to question why and certainly not to place yourself in the role of judge and jury, regardless of what you as another human being, think. As stated before, your opinions do not matter and are not relevant.

Indeed you are likely to hear of callers, both male and female in case you were wondering, who are seeing more people than just having the perennial 'affair'. We do not know their motivation but if they are calling you it is (perhaps not surprisingly) because they need some help and guidance. Again, it is for you to tell them honestly and supportively the truth as it is given to you.

The other main area callers ask about is their work and career. This may be whether they will get the job they have applied for or whether they should give up their job in the supermarket stacking shelves to follow their dream of becoming a brain surgeon or airline pilot – ok, so this may be an exaggeration but you will be surprised by how many times this principle comes out in a reading – and in my experience the answer is mostly yes – what else is life for if it is not to push ourselves to excel, be the best we can be and pursue our dreams?

Indeed as I write this I am reminded of a reading I gave where this happened. The caller was working in a debt-collection office and I could see from her cards that she clearly struggled with what her essentially caring nature was and having to push people to repay money and generally take a strict and 'hard-line' approach with them. I suggested this, with which she readily agreed and then told her that I could see in her cards she had an unfulfilled dream dating perhaps back to childhood that was still with her. When she finished gasping she told me in an excited tone that she always wanted to be a midwife but never thought she would be capable. From what I could see, she would make one hell of a midwife!

So when dealing with work and career issues be clear again and stick to your truth. I would suggest also especially to be open to the unexpected. People can and do make drastic career changes into things they themselves never thought they would do. Just make the suggestions you can see for them and even if they laugh or dismiss it out of hand, stick to what you see for them. It can often be a case of sowing seeds and so many times I have either had myself or heard callers coming back to a reader and saying that they had indeed dismissed what they suggested at the time only to find that they were offered something in that field or saw a course for it, or whatever and were very happy they did so.

Just as many callers will give you a specific question or at least area of their life, be it relationship, work, children and so on for you to sick your proverbial psychic teeth into, an equal number will just request a .general reading'. As stated elsewhere there is usually something behind this but we are being client-led, as is the best approach for our work and so a general reading we will give.

Do not mistake this for giving our generalised information that is not specific to them and their individuality and situation. Our information must still be specific, honest and offer them something they did not know already or have access to. A general reading requires that we give them some information on the different main areas of their lives, again relationships, work, home life etc.

Once you go into whatever area they really want to know about they will say something in response and the remainder of the reading will most likely be about this. Whether you work with Tarot, Runes or any kind of tool or none at all, the structure required to give to your readings here is to spend a few minutes dealing first with one part of your caller's life, give all the information you have on this, ask if they have any questions on this area before you move, respond to these if they do, then move on to the next area of life, invite questions on this and so on. This way you are likely to hit on what they really want as well as succeeding in their stated request. This will also easily take you 20 minutes thus ensuring you give them value for their money as well as maximising on your call duration and of course, earnings. Everybody's happy!

This is also the approach to take if the caller responds to you when you ask them what they want a reading on or about with a 'nothing really' kind of reply. If they give you nothing to work with, work with everything. Be confident enough to take control of the process and tell them you will look at the different areas of their life and they can ask any questions as you go. Get stuck in, get involved and give them a reading that will amaze as well as help them. They will get the help and guidance they need and, over and above the few pounds you will earn, you will gain a sense of satisfaction knowing what you've just done for another human being. It can be easy to sarcastically refer here to that 'warm glow within' but you really will get it and believe me, it feels good! To be a good telephone psychic, you have to love it, there is no place for doing this work from only a sense of duty.

ONE-QUESTION CALLS

Other callers will have something very specific and will want only that and will (often forcefully) declare this right at the start of the reading. That is of course their prerogative and is perfectly fine, but can be hard for us poor readers to jump straight in and do this in under 10 seconds! Whilst we can and indeed should respond to this one question for them, they can often come across in their immediacy as wanting you to get on with it and they will be off just as soon as you've given then your answer. This may be the case and again is their right, but you must be strong and clear enough not to be drawn into a rushed response and an unclear reading that can be its result.

Instead politely explain to them that you will do that for them but it is not an instant response and your initial information may not cover this, just for the first minute or so, whilst you make your link psychically to them. If you are clear, calm and truthful they will usually accept this and relax more. If they do not they will probably hang up and if they do, they do! On the assumption however that our dear caller is still on the line, let's take a look at how to deal with their one question fully and properly.

Many readers can struggle with giving a reading lasting more than a few minutes when given this dilemma, the result more often than enough being dissatisfaction on the part of both customer and reader. We know that as a professional reader you want to give a full and complete reading that befits your status and reputation. Equally, this is what the caller requires, whether they realise this or not. It now befalls you to show them this, which you will do with the professionalism of your approach and the accuracy and relevancy of the information you give them.

Very often callers will tell you they only want to know about one thing and nothing else. There can clearly be a defence mechanism at work here, the fear of hearing the truth and facing what they fear being the prime cause of this. If, as the reader you take the approach of acknowledging their request and setting about giving that full reading, almost without concern for the time it takes, you will find that they will respond and open up to you and a full twenty minute reading will ensue and indeed fly by, just as it should.

The principle here really is that the caller has a right to a full reading, not a diluted shadow of what you can really do. It is your task to take their one question or subject and place this in the context of the whole of their self and life. We cannot separate our life into compartments that easily. If you just take charge of the process of the reading and once you have looked into the part of their life simply continue on to how this will affect the next area and so on, they will want to hear what you have to say and they will leave being aware of a bigger picture and more informed than when you began. In this way you have fulfilled your part of the deal, giving them information they would not otherwise have accessed and the rest is up to them. They can of course end the call at any time they wish and if they do, so be it, but you will have the knowledge that you could have done no more and this is important to acknowledge.

So it is really about getting to the root cause of their problem or the underlying nature of their situation. Any good psychic worth their crystal ball will be able to see this from a reading. It can be helpful when dealt a one question reading to explain to the caller that you will certainly look at that for them and see what choices and options may be there for them and what the likely outcome is, so that you will empower them and help them get or keep what they want.

Do be aware of the language you are using, keeping a positive slant on things and offering them choices, opinions and decisions. In this way you engage with them and the reading is a two-way process, as all psychic readings should be. Bring the conversation to their level and mirror back to them what they have said. This means for example that when they have just told you that they feel trapped ion their marriage and that their husband no longer 'does it' for them, you respond with something like 'so you feel as if your marriage is holding you back and that your husband does not offer an exciting attraction now'. They will of course agree and you can continue by looking at the cards or whatever to see what response or course of action is indicated. They will want to see this and so from an opening 'one-question' such as 'will my marriage end' you have already opened up into all kinds of possible futures with them, whether with or without the husband. Now your problem becomes dealing with the fullness of this in just 20 minutes!

It can also be good to ask your caller open-ended questions in response to what you have told them. These are questions that do not elicit a yes or no response, but that asks for thoughts, feelings and so on – e.g. 'how do you feel about that'. This process will also strengthen the connection between you on a psychic level and the caller will hear that you are taking an active interest in them, rather than just telling them information. Use of their name regularly will also help with this.

Some readers feel that if the client knows what they want and tells them so at the start of the reading they should give them an answer immediately. We should be clear here that nothing in life is ever that black or white and this will not get their real issue dealt with and answered. There is a profound and audible sense of disappointment when you give them only a little more than a simple yes or no and the call invariably closes- usually with them picking up the 'phone to ask their question of another reader in the hope they will get their issue responded to this time.

We should make the point here that the above strategies and techniques are not given to keep the caller on the 'phone any longer than they wish or choose to be there. The sole motivation here is to offer them the best that you are capable of, give them the best reading possible and help them to help themselves, as should be the goal of every psychic to their customers. The above methods will let the client know that they matter, their issues and real and important, they are an individual with needs that you can help them meet. They will finish with you informed, empowered and uplifted by these things.

This of course all increases the likelihood of them calling you again and even becoming a regular caller, with you as their resident psychic. You will be pleased with this, so will they and so will the company you are working with. In short, everybody wins!

OVER-USE AND DEPENDENCY

This does however raise another issue that can unfortunately become an all too common one, I suspect not only on telephone psychic lines both such and similar services. This is over-use of the service that can result in an unhealthy dependency and even addiction. Please make yourself aware of the PhonePay Plus regulations in regard to this as there are clear guidelines that you have a responsibility to meet and uphold.

Essentially these state that if you become aware that a caller is using the service too often you should raise this issue. This should be done both with to the company you work with and the caller themselves. Any company will be able to place a block on a caller telephone number (though of course this can be got around) or be able to make their readers aware of the caller and instruct them not to give readings to them.

It should also be explained to your too-regular caller that you are not able to offer them a reading until perhaps another month has gone by or something definite has shifted or changed for them and their situation. If and when they ask why it should be explained to them that under the regulations governing live telephone services you cannot permit calls from the same person too often as this is regarded as an abuse of their position. As a psychic it is often wise to add to this that until a passage of time goes by or something significant changes in their life or situation, you cannot give them any further information and it would be morally wrong of you to simply repeat yourself and not give them value for money.

There is also the issue of cost and the caller's ability to afford the cost of every call they make. Too many calls in a short space of time soon builds up and a surprisingly large amount of money owing to the telephone company can accrue easily into four figures. The cost of each call should be explained to the caller and irrespective of their stated ability to afford the calls, it is your responsibility to suggest and if necessary insist that they wait a month before calling again, or give them a compromise of 2 calls per month or whatever seems appropriate given their previous level of usage and the particular aspects of their individual situation.

My experience has usually been here that the caller will usually admit to over-using the service and concern about the cost of it all. Should they struggle with this then you and should make referral to a telephone counselling service or if necessary The Samaritans. Whether they choose to follow this up is not your responsibility or even concern but does ensure that you have fulfilled your obligation. You will have also given them other options for support if they are truly in need.

So there we can safely leave our valued and lovely customer. They come in all shapes and sizes and with every problem, question or situation you can imagine and several you probably cannot! They can and will be by turns delightful, fascinating, funny, clever, heart-breaking, despairing, flirty, tragic, rude, insulting, obnoxious and even pathetic. Whatever they may be it is not yours to question and certainly not to judge. Do your very best through your readings to guide and help them and give each and every one 100%, for certainly each and every one requires and deserves this. The rest is simply, nothing to do with you.

CHAPTER 4 – THE BUSINESS

At this point in our proceedings we must take a look at the nature and form of the telephone psychic business, or industry as it has become. Here we will see that it is just that, a business and like any other it is geared towards one thing – profit. This point should be made abundantly clear and strong from the outset.

This is said because many psychics, mediums and readers are spiritually minded folk who can find it somewhat distasteful to be making a profit from people who just want some help and guidance. Whilst it is true to say that the customers do indeed want that guidance and help, and as psychics we are the ones who can give it to them, it is equally true to say that, the world being what it is, money must exchange hands for this to happen.

If it helps, you can see this monetary exchange as a form of energy flow that enables the customer to get what they need, as indeed it surely is. The energy here takes the form of money and some of it will come your way.

I have known some readers who think and can take resentment to the idea that they are being paid something of a pittance given the amount the customer has paid for the reading, whilst the fat cats in the office are paid large salaries and the company sits back and soaks up the profits. It may have been the case a decade ago that there was good money to be made from this business and many did, including readers. The world is now a different place financially however and this is no longer true of any telephone psychic company that I know.

The hourly rate paid to readers is often above that of those carrying out the administration work, as arguably it should be; that's a matter for each individual. Rest assured however, readers are always valued very highly and a good, reliable and punctual reader can quite easily select which company they work with, such sadly, is their rarity. Telephone Psychic Companies will always look to improve their readers if they can and a long list of regular callers you can bring to their lines will be welcomed with open arms.

The relationship between reader and company is really a symbiotic one where each depends on the other for their success and indeed existence. Anyone taking a contrary or superior view in this will soon find themselves proven wrong. In terms of earnings, you can be equally assured that the company will be doing what and all it can to bring as many calls in for you as possible – why wouldn't they? You can also be sure that they will know that the rest is up to you.

By giving good quality, accurate and professional readings each and every time and not lapsing into bad habits from over-familiarity or plain boredom, the company will see and expect you to take responsibility for the generation of your own income. This is done by the creation of a regular and loyal band of callers who will stick with you. After the past 13 or so years this has been proven to me over and over again and readers who can do this are the backbone and life of the company they work with.

HOW IT HAPPENS

Now that we have got the pecking order clear let's step back a little and look at the construction of the business. Following on from our opening financial salvo let's cast our eyes over how the whole thing works. I have known many readers who form the impression that all they have to do is be there and answer the phone, talk for a while and wait for the money to appear. As said before, if that is your view, please leave now, you'll find me holding the door open for you!

In order for a call to appear magically in your comfy, warm reading room, much has to take place. First, the company, once formed, ratified and registered must purchase or lease a complex and expensive telephone set-up. This technology was new during the 1980's and as with all such technology, is prone to development, changes, malfunctions and breakdowns. A specialist company must then be part of the set-up, or knowledgeable staff employed to deal with such things. Often they will need to be on call at all hours if your company is a 24 hour set-up.

The telephony system will need to be able to handle any number of calls that may be received at any one time, identify which of possibly several hundred numbers has been dialled and then re-route or direct this incoming call via a further outgoing call that it makes, to the next correct reader in the queue, based on certain criteria is has been given, which can be many and complex.

This little miracle then makes your telephone ring. When you do this, the system then connects you with the caller, having played you both a message to tell you this. It then supports and records your call and pops in to remind you when you are running out of time. Once you've finished it will then make a note of exactly how long your call lasted, charge the caller appropriately and allocate your portion of the money owing to you. If you're lucky it will give you a five minute break until it will give you another call, as it cares about you enough to know you need a wee and want a drink!

For the customer to make that call they must have first found out about the service. These days, this will either have been from a website or from a magazine or newspaper advert. So the website must be designed, checked and promoted up the various search engines and continually refined and checked to achieve maximum viewing potential and optimisation, as the term now has it. Trust me, this is no easy task, especially when, as happened a few years ago, the largest and most effective search engine in the world throws a curve ball into the system (in cricketing terms this would of course have been a 'googlie'!) which literally over-night re-defined how the whole thing works.

Adverts must also be defined and placed, edited, checked and approved and often altered to again meet strict publishing and regulatory criteria, often with deadlines well ahead of appearance.

Deals must also be struck with publishing houses to carry advertisements on an exclusive basis, which often requires back-bending of a kind any accomplished yogi would be proud of!

Now the simple preliminaries are in place the customer can make a call and you can give them a reading. This is of course, after the pc system to operate it has been designed and implemented, staff employed and trained, and somewhere to house the little lot found and paid for. Once this has been done a team of readers must also be found, trained, website profile and photo set-up and a system of payment from the customer established, as well as one to pay you!

COMPANIES

Since the technology to do so came into existence in the 1990's a great many companies and individuals have set themselves up as a telephone psychic service. Many companies, seeming to focus around one city in particular for some reason (which shall remain nameless to protect this author!) soon earned a reputation for, shall we say, not being authentic. The basic remit given to readers here was to hand them a Tarot deck and book, place 'readers' in an office and tell them to keep callers on the line as long as possible. Fortunately, although such companies probably still exist, they are no longer the norm and certainly not the focus of this book.

So we shall move on and take a look at the plethora of reputable companies and operations that do now exist. To attempt to provide a survey or even an overview of individual companies and their methods would be somewhat futile, since they are forever changing, in their practices, promotions and methods. What we can do however is provide some information to look for and consider when it comes to which company, or companies you choose to work with.

Although many companies will have deals with various magazines and publications by far the most common method of finding telephone psychic companies is by internet search. Obviously there are a good many internet search engines out there but whichever you chose you are sure to find more than enough to choose from.

The 'home page' of each company will of course be geared towards enticing clients to call for a reading so it may well be that you need to search a little to find the contact you need. Look for a link that mentions 'jobs', 'working with us', 'becoming a reader' and this kind of thing generally. This may require looking at the dreaded small print but it may well save you questions and time later on.

As mentioned before most, and arguably by default of doing so the best, will require one or more test readings from you before accepting you as a reader. Some however do not and these tend to place more reliance on your abilities speaking for themselves, or not as the case may be! Indeed it is an increasingly popular approach, brought about by the advent of new technologies and customer demands and expectations, that the set-up and operational structure of telephone psychic companies places the emphasis son the reader to generate their own business.

Before we look at this a little more, let me first encourage you to satisfy yourself as to the requirements of the Company for their readers. Usually the majority of this information will, or should be, available somewhere on their website, but if not it may be that you need to hunt down a 'Customer Service' or 'Contact Us' page and establish a connection with them first. It can be a good idea to be clear first about what you need to know.

HOW MUCH?

Chief among these will of course be the payment you will receive. This will be a 'per minute' rate for all of your calls. Mostly this will be a flat rate, possibly higher if the reading has been paid for by debit or credit card, the reason being that there is a greater profit margin from these than the premium rate calls. Some companies will pay one rate for booked calls, another for premium rate. Other companies may have more of a tiered payment structure, whereby the longer your calls last, the higher the 'per-minute' rate goes. Of course this can be a good incentive for long calls but from the readers' perspective, this should not be the motivation. As I have told many a reader over the years, if you concentrate on giving the best reading you are capable of, the duration of the calls will look after themselves and you will find that you naturally fall into the higher bracket of payment for them. If callers are getting a good reading they will be quite happy to stay on the line, without you trying to extend it artificially, which callers will know instantly and you will not hear from them again.

Along with how much you will earn from each call you will also need to ascertain the frequency of payment. Companies will either pay monthly, which the majority will do, but there are some that will pay you weekly. Those that do pay weekly however usually pay a lower rate. Before you dismiss them though, be aware of the practical uses a weekly amount can have.

You will also need to determine by what method you will be paid. It is usual now for companies to pay straight into your bank account but be clear about what date of the month this will be and how long after you have earned the money you will receive it. There are some companies that pay one month in arrears to the end of the previous month, so for instance what you earn say to the end of March you will not receive until the end of April. Others will have a cut of date of say, the last Sunday of a month and will pay you the following week. This is simply to allow the finance department of a larger company time to 'do their thing' notify the bank and then have the requisite banking time of 3 working days to process your money through their own systems.

Do be careful if a company insists that the only way they will pay you is by cheque, a process which gives you no control and fosters a sense of uncertainty each time it comes around to payday. The possibilities of human error creeping in to such a system are increased, both in terms of errors on the cheque itself (mostly the amount!) and with the postal service delaying getting it to you. You then have to find a time when you can get to the bank and then waiting the statutory period for the cheque to clear, usually 5 or 7 working days.
It is also sensible at this stage to establish that the Company will send you some kind of statement showing your income. Mostly this will be by the previously mentioned 'self-bill invoice'. You will need some kind of statement for your own accounting purposes, but such a statement should also be itemised. That is to say it should show a breakdown of all the calls you have done in that pay period. Ideally this should show the exact length of the call and therefore the amount you earned from it.

This allows you to double-check the Companies figures with your own, which you will have of course compiled from each and every call you took, as I have recommended previously. Your records need to show the date, time and length of each call, plus the callers' name and date of birth, along with any notes you care to make to jog your memory. These checks are not there because you do not trust your Company, but simply as a check so you know everything is as it should be.

Even in the most automated system mistakes can and do occur and it is best if these are brought to light as soon as possible. They are rare and in my experience, with a good Company never intentional. This could mean you were under-paid or even over-paid. Either way, you will need to bring this to the attention of the Company so it can be straightened out. In the unlikely event of your being over-paid do not think it will not get spotted and it's your lucky day. That is not the way of good conscience and it is highly likely that it will come to light at a later date and will be deducted from the next payment due to you, which could create difficulties for you. Equally, if you are under-paid, you will want what is owing to you as soon as possible.

THE RIGHT ROTA

Next comes the question of when you will work. Different companies will have different expectations and minimum requirements. It may be that a Company will allow you to work without a rota at all and you can simply log on and take calls whenever you wish. Whilst this has the advantage of giving you freedom to choose your working hours to suit you, allowing you to dip in and out, determine how long you stay logged-on for on each shift, even arrange a follow-up call at a certain time with your regulars, the disadvantage is that there is no control over how many readers may be logged on at any one time. There more there are of course, the less chance there is of each of you receiving a call.

Other companies will require you to be logged on for a minimum of however many hours, usually per week. This can be as little as 8 or may be more than double this. Do check also if your Company has any requirements as to when you need to be logged on. Some companies will insist that either so many of your regular hours must be at the same time each week or that some must be evenings or until midnight (or later) at least once per week and some hours must cove a shift at the weekends and so on. Before you baulk at this, remember that the days of the great majority of people working just 9 to 5 hours are gone and people are now free of work at all times of the day, evening and indeed night. It is when people are not at work they will of course call for readings so it makes good business sense for you to be available at least some of what can still be called 'unsocial hours', as well as during the day in the week.

I would also recommend that you give serious consideration to devoting some regular time each week that you stick to and will be on regularly, come rain, shine, snuffles, hangovers, sick pets. Or many of the other maladies that confront us all. Regular callers are the life-blood of your business and income and they will want and need you to be reliable, knowing they can literally, call on you when they need to. These callers are unlikely to stay on line for an hour each time and nor should they but short, regular calls you may come to rely on as much as they rely on you. If you can give at least one or two regular shifts each and every week when such people will know you will be there it can be a massive advantage and go a long way to your keeping these customers rather than losing to another reader.

I would suggest then that you calculate in your own mind when you are willing and truthfully able to work, as a starting point at least and look to find a Company that will by and large match your requirements. Of course there may need to be flexibility on both a sides, at least a little, so do bear this in mind but if you are prepared to be so, you will find that most good Companies will recognise and support this and be equally yoga-like for you in their approach.

By way of conclusion to this little segment, the importance of sticking to your agreed rota time should also be stressed. Once you have built up a number of regular callers this need will become apparent. You also need to avoid establishing a reputation of being unreliable with the Company you work with as this can have repercussions. Your regulars may plan to call you when they are expecting you to be on and will soon lose faith if you do not appear. It can be all too easy when you are sitting at home nursing a lovely cup of coffee in front of your favourite tv drama or film when it comes to 'logging-on time' to think that you need not bother or won't be missed.

As I found to much merriment over the years of managing these services readers are quite adept at coming up with all manner of weird and wonderful reasons why they simply cannot log on for their shift. Simply for enjoyment and with a platitude of 'don't be like this', here are a select of few of, I promise, all quite genuine reasons given for not logging on, apart from the ubiquitous car-breakdowns, 'phone mishaps, lost diaries and hangovers –

There are mice in the loft
My neighbours son has a splinter in his finger
There are sheep in the garden
My spray tan hasn't dried and I can't put the 'phone to my ear
They aren't mice, they're rats in the loft
There are cows in the garden

and lastly and best of all –

I've run out of mandrake root and have to go to Marrakesh to buy some more!!

TECHNOLOGICAL TERRORS

Since the 1990's when the telephone psychic industry began there have been significant advances in the technology available to such services. Apart from improvements in the performance of sophisticated telephony systems, (aside from the universally annoying Menus we have to now endure each time we call any big company) other progressions have occurred which add to the remit and scope of the bigger and more established telephone psychic companies.

These advances are such that the term 'telephone psychic company' should perhaps now be redefined as 'online psychic services' since this is what they are becoming. It could be worthwhile debating the merits and ethics of such services but in many ways this would something of a pointless waste of precious time, since the rights and/or wrongs of such things rarely become considered in human history. We have a tendency to do something because we can and have the capability to, irrespective of whether we actually should or not. So it is additional means and methods to the telephone, of providing psychic readings are now the norm.

Readings are now routinely offered via webcam, which may send some readers screaming in terror and running for the hills at the thought of being seen. It must be said here that I have known of some readers who sit up in bed and do their readings. Essentially there is nothing wrong with this when it comes to telephone readings only. However it should be obvious that this is wholly inappropriate if the reader can be seen by the caller via a webcam. If nothing else we do need to be sure that it is absolutely clear just what service is being offered here!

Most online psychic services now offer the facility to connect with their chosen reader by telephone as well as webcam. Once you have been set-up by a company on their 'platform' and your details are available on their website, there is usually a button to click for the customer to make their call by their chosen method.

Most personal computers, be they laptops or desktops, come supplied with a webcam. If they don't they are now easily available for little cost – which as with all things will vary, so do look about first. Technical specifications can vary of course, but the vast majority of webcams will be acceptable for all online psychic services and the quality of even a basic webcam acceptable for these purposes.

On the assumption that you have no objection to your customers being able to see you, it follows that you will need to give some thought to what they will see. First comes your own appearance and you should take clear to be professional looking, without going over the top and 'power-dressing' and so appearing cold, calculating and too 'business-like' Basically a 'smart, casual' appearance is preferable. Whatever else you may choose, let us hope that you do not don a headscarf, drape a cloth over a lamp and try and look like some kind of 'Gypsy Rose-Lee' archetype! Be yourself and the rest will follow.

Do consider your surroundings as well. The customer's focus will be mostly on you of course but during the course of their reading they will have opportunity to have a little look around where you are. Obviously you should not move around while doing the reading, but some readers are quite mobile in their chair. Ensure that you adjust the webcam so that you are still fully visible and have not half-disappeared of the screen. Most webcams show you a small display in the corner of what the customer sees, so keep an eye on this occasionally.

One idea you might like to explore is having a banner or picture behind you that describes your readings or having an inspiring image or picture. Many psychics these days have a scroll-banner on display when they attend psychic fairs and the like and this could work well here as wll. Do ensure however that your personal 'phone number to contact details are not on display. Apart from not knowing what kind of person may then continually pester you with calls at all hours of the day, it will break the regulations of the Company you work with and could lead to your dismissal from their ranks.

A great advantage of the webcam link between you and the caller applies mostly to the Tarot readers, this being of course the possibility of the seeing the cards you are reading. Some care needs to be taken with this of course. You should avoid the tendency to shove each and every card in front of the webcam and holding out an unsteady hand for too long a time, so they can scrutinise a somewhat shaky image. Do remember that the customer is most likely paying on a per-minute rate or will have booked for a specific amount of time and they will not appreciate half of it being taken up by just being shown cards – it is information they want and most will not care what cards it comes from.

That said there are times in the dynamics of a reading when it is especially useful for the customer to see the card in question. This may be to point out a specific symbol or image on it, or to show the difference between one card and the next and so on. Time and experience will show you when this is appropriate, but tell the caller why you are showing them this card and once they have responded, put the card down and get on with the reading.

This can certainly keep them interested and engaged, so long as it is not abused. All callers are very well aware when they are being 'short-changed' in anyway and this kind of information on your feedback you can do without. Lastly, don't forget to smile when you are on webcam!

In addition to readings via webcam many psychic services are now offering a 'chat' facility to their armoury of offerings. This is chat in a typed sense. The basic structure here is that the customer is at their pc, as will you be, and having clicked on your pin, or the box enabling them to do this via the Company's website, this instigates a pop-up box appearing on your screen. There is often an automated first telling them the per-minute cost of the chat, along with something to confirm your name, pin and perhaps list of your skills. You will also usually be shown the customer's name, or at least the name they have registered under on the website.

It is for you then to begin giving them a typed reading. For these it is best to begin with just a short sentence, which you might like to have ready in a 'Word' file to copy and paste. This saves valuable time and enables you to get stuck in straight away, rather than appearing that you are just keeping them going for as long as possible to prolong your connection with them and so your fee. As mentioned before, customers are all too aware of ths ploy when it is could be used, so it is good to assure them this way that you are there to help them and wish to get into their reading without undue delay.

That said, you do of course need to establish what they want from you, or from their reading. So your pre-ordained' sentence may read something like this:

Hi, welcome to the psychic service, my name is Fred and my pin is 0007, I am a Tarot reader and clairvoyant, working with my spirit guide to help you. What would you like a reading about today?

You will of course then receive a reply and away you go. You may like to again have a sentence ready to say something along the lines of:

That's fine, I will just tune in and deal some cards on this for you, I will just be a few seconds

What you then need to do is take only a few seconds to do this and begin typing back to them, with your information. A swift shuffle of cards will suffice, dealing them however you usually do and start. In most services of this kind the technology enables the customer to see when you are typing, although they cannot see what until you hit 'send or whatever button is required on the set-up.

You need to avoid typing one large paragraph, just a couple of short sentences so that this kind of reading happens via a two-way dialogue. It is a little different than a voice reading but if you are confident you will soon adjust. It can be helpful to help the flow of readings and to ensure that your customer is getting what they want and need from their reading to conclude each, or most, replies that you give with a question. This can just be 'do you understand this, or 'does this make sense' or something along these lines. If however it is more specific that's fine, so long as your question relates to what you are saying.

Once you have dealt with one subject fully it is fine then to take a lead with the reading just as with telephone techniques. Here you can then say something like' ok, that's all I have on this subject, before I move on to (insert the next thing you are getting information on, which you should be able to do) do you have any questions or something you want me to focus on? This naturally takes the reading further and shows you have more information for them, whilst making it clear that you can be led by them and they have opportunity to say what they wish.

Of course you will need to be at least a reasonable typist, but with practice even the most basic of typing skills will get swifter, so if you are new to it, take a little time between calls to practice your typing. Simply sit and type whatever comes to you – you never know, you might find yourself writing an article that can be published somewhere or, heaven help you, even a book! However quick or slow you may be, do take the time for a quick read of what you have written before you send it. Typos have a nasty habit of creeping in even when you think you are fully accurate, even for the best of copy typists. Of course the character of typos is that they can end up with some unfortunate word or expression that could convey a quite different meaning to what you intended – it can take a difference of just one letter to present the worst of 'Freudian slips' to your unsuspecting customer!

When you reading comes to its natural end, you may again like to have a ready-made sentence to sign off with. A further suggestion for you here is:

'Thanks for contacting me, it's been a pleasure to read for you and I hope it has helped you. Feel free to contact me again when you would like to, my pin again is 0007. Good luck with everything and very best wishes, Fred'

Astute readers will have noticed that the style of typing employed here is that of doing so just as if you are talking to the client by telephone. If you have your mind-set this way, you will not go far wrong. Approach 'chat' readings with this in mind and you will come across as sincere and genuine, as well as professional but approachable and friendly. All these qualities are vital for an effective and fulfilling experience for the customer, which as always, is the most important thing. Not just for them of course but for your own professionalism, attracting the customer back to you and enhancing the chances of good and positive feedback they may leave you.

IT'S THE LAW

It is a sad fact, in my view, that we now live in a litigious society. So much so that for some this is how they make their living. Of course those who are fake, rip people off or deliberately mislead or abuse others should be accountable for their actions. Whilst you may believe and accept that this will be done karmically (with which I agree), this holds no sway in any legal setting.

So it is that Consumer Protection Regulations now exist with which you must ensure you comply. This applies irrespective of whether you agree with what you must do or not – to not do so would be folly and you would most certainly regret it in the (however unlikely) event of your being taken to Court for any reason.
Depending on your level of concern about this, you may like to obtain documents from the Office of Fair Trading (for the UK) at www.oft.gov.uk, concerning 'consumer protection from unfair trading'. I would also strongly recommend you avail yourself of membership of an organisation such as the Spiritual Workers Association (www.theswa.org.uk) which has much helpful information and campaigns in this and other related fields. Membership here is just a few pounds per month and has many advantages.

The regulations introduced in 2008, against much outcry from many in the field, resulted in the requirement of all psychic readers to have a disclaimer in their literature attesting that their readings are 'for entertainment purposes only. If you look at a number of psychics' websites, as well as different telephone psychic companies' sites, you will find as many variations on the wording required. Some produce a length paragraph which is mostly seemingly meaningless legal jargon. Others stick with the simple 'All readings are for entertainment purposes only.

What matters is that the customer is made aware that their reading does not constitute legal advice or have any legal and certainly medical standing. When it comes specifically to Mediumship the disclaimer appears to need to include mention that is it a 'scientific experiment' in which the customer willingly participates of their own accord. Whatever wording is used, do look at the Company you work with that they have something along these lines displayed. There is not a requirement for you to state this yourself at the start of every call/chat you receive, as long as the statement is available to the customer beforehand.

Regardless of your individual opinion on such regulations and their resulting requirements do be aware that they also play a role in protecting you, as well as our erstwhile consumer. In practice I have found that it works that everyone knows that they are not having a reading just for entertainment purposes but will accept that the law says we need to say this. The approach often taken has the attitude of 'ok, we gotta say this so now it's said, let's forget about it and get on with it'.

As mentioned before, in the unlikely event of someone trying to sue you for whatever legal reason that can muster up, you will find that the regulations serve to give you credence as well and should provide a healthy, non-biased structure for the matter to be dealt with. So, it seems very wise to check that your Company is aware of and adheres to these regulations, join the SWA for your own peace of mind if nothing else (you will be strengthening the position of every spiritual worker/psychic if you do, as well as yourself), then get on with the business you have chosen to make your own and stick to the highest standards of authenticity and transparency you can.

THE FINAL ACCOUNT

I mentioned before that without exception, so far as I am aware, all telephone psychics are self-employed and I dealt with what this basically entails in order to establish yourself as such. Now that you have become a fully-fledged and we hope successful telephone psychic, you need to ensure that as a self-employed person you file all the right and of course, accurate accounts.

If you are adept at such things, it is possible to complete sufficient self-employment accounts at the end of each year. It is hard these days to avoid knowing when they are necessary as once you have registered you can be sure there will be a veritable flood of 'public service announcement's issuing forth from the relevant government office, telling you to avoid fine, the rack, the iron maiden and other devices if you do not get your accounts in on time for them to see how much of your hard-earned pennies they can filter away!

In order to this not just timeously but also to your own best advantage, it will be necessary to maintain financial records through the year. This way you will have pretty much all the information you require when it comes to the completion of the dreaded Tax Return. The records necessary for this may be simpler than you think and although a little lengthy and seemingly complicated, completion of a tax return need not fill you with stress and reaching swiftly for the nearest alcoholic beverage of psychiatrist's couch once done!

Your necessary financial records can essentially be done via two 'Excel' Spreadsheets (assuming you, like the majority of humanity today, work with a pc that operates using the Windows system). One spreadsheet shows your income, one shows your expenditure.

The income is simple, particularly so if telephone psychic reading is your only work. You will receive either a weekly or monthly amount and this should be entered for your income. You will be issued with some kind of statement to prove this by the Company you work with and this should always be retained as proof of income. To this end, always seek to have some kind of paper proof of anything and everything that you enter into your accounts. In the (unfortunately increasingly highly likely) event of the Tax Office wishing to 'investigate' your accounts, you may be required to provide such proof of all the figures you have given. If you have it, no problem, if you don't, it can cost you!

For expenditure it is worth getting informed upon. There is a great deal that you can claim as tax-deductible expense. What this means is that the total amount of tax allowable expenses you incur during a year is taken away from the total of your income. The resulting figure is the one then used to calculate how much tax you pay, so it is most certainly, clearly and definitely quite literally in your interest to add everything in that can that you are legally allowed to claim for. Hopefully the over-use of adjectives in that last sentence will have proven to you that you need to do this!

It may be worth your while, and if you have any doubts as to your capability in this area then I highly recommend it, in using an accountant to do the job of all this for you. Of course this will cost you but it may well be the case that the amount you pay the accountant is less than the amount you would have paid in unnecessary tax than if you did not have them! It is of course worthwhile looking and asking around for a recommendation for an accountant and hopefully you will find someone who is aware of the work of a psychic and so what can and cannot be claimed.
Once you have one, you will find a good accountant to be a deep well of useful information about many aspects of running your business and since are paying them for this, do not be afraid to use them and ask all the questions you have.
Also, never hold back on giving them information. From the accountants' point of view, if you do not tell them something or provide the information, they cannot act on it. If they do not need it, they will not berate you for it, so have no fear. They will just ignore it, but anything that saves you money is worth trying so give them everything!

So, while you are beavering away at your work you are in the habit of recording your financial operations as you go, all ready to either complete your won tax return or provide your trusty accountant with when he summons them. Income itself is fairly simple, as mentioned above. Expenditure can be a little different, with what you can and cannot claim for.

Since you are working from home you are entitled to claim an allowance on use of home as office. This amount can also include a percentage of your utility bills (gas/electric/water etc.) since you cannot work without them. Think also of the equipment you need to do your work, all of which are tax deductible - a desk to work at, table to do your readings on, chair(s) to sit on, suitable lighting for this, a telephone headset system, a pc and all that goes with it, stationery, any travel you carry out for work related purposes, subsistence while doing so (meals/drinks, accommodation), postage, Tarot cards, crystal ball, candles, incense and more besides. Basically anything that you spend money as part of your work, in whatever sense, is allowable as an expense. These all contribute, down to the last penny, in reducing the amount of tax you are legally required to pay from the heard-earned, £6 per reading that you can effuse blood, sweat and tears over.

Taking the time to compile this information as you go, however laborious and a drudge it may seem, is worth your doing. If you are totally unable to do it yourself, get someone to do it for you, even if it means you have to pay them something to do. Get in the habit of keeping a till receipt of all your purchases. Then go through them and consider if it is a work expense. You may be surprised at what is, and indeed what isn't!

CHAPTER 5 – THE CAREER

The majority of telephone psychic companies were established in the early to mid-1990s and the best of these are still going. Many have come and gone and doubtless still will, as some more unscrupulous folk seek to jump on the bandwagon and make money quick. However the days of this are largely gone now and it is the strong few that survive long-term. Given the right structure of a company, run sensibly both to provide the customer with a genuine and positive experience and fulfil a profitable enterprise for the readers, it is possible now to see the work of a telephone psychic as a career – or at least a part of it.

One Company I worked with for 11 years had been established about 3 years prior to my joining. Some readers had been there since its inception and are still there now. Many others that joined in the first few years of my work there are also still working with them, all having established an excellent reputation with many regular callers. So it is from this that we can see the possibility of establishing a career, at least in part, as a telephone psychic.

In my experience of this, being a telephone psychic is rarely a readers full-time occupation. It must be said that for those that are, there is a continuing, grave danger of becoming stale, losing ones' enthusiasm and therefore 'spark' for each and every reading, which must be protected and nurtured. The great majority of telephone psychics have many strings to their proverbial bows, by way of giving private readings, appearances at Psychic Fairs and so on, plus teaching in their chosen 'specialised subject'.

So perhaps the most balanced view and approach as a telephone psychic is to see it as a career yes, but not to put all one's eggs in one basket, in terms of working only with one Company as well as this being your only source of income. Many psychics incorrectly assume that they can only work for one Company. As a self-employed person the manner of operation here is that you have a product – in this case psychic readings. The who, how and when you choose to place that product with is entirely your choice. Of course loyalty can play a part here as it should do, but working with one Company can be a limiting restriction on your activities and an unnecessary one to boot.

It should be mentioned here that it is of course totally unacceptable to be working with more than one Company simultaneously, by which I mean being logged on to two different Companies' system at the same time. This may and I hope does, sound obvious to say, but I have seen this done. Of course as soon as you receive a call from one line you cannot then receive another for the other line. The only thing likely to happen here is that as soon as it is realised you are missing calls you are highly likely to be removed from both lines. Be aware that many people in the industry do know each other and do communicate – word gets round as they say and once a bad reputation is established, like a flea to a dog, it can be very hard to shake off!

ONWARDS AND UPWARDS

Given that what may have started as a nice little idea to earn yourself some extra income could now be part of your career as a fully-fledged, professional psychic, there can be a need to consider this so it is done properly, both for yourself and your long-suffering customers. Any work where we are dealing primarily with people, their lives and problems requires that we always be the best we can possibly be and this can make and create many issues.

Chief among these is how avoid the staleness that can so easily beset the telephone psychic who sits at his desk, cards in hand and dutifully answers the telephone when it rings, day in, day out. To positively respond to this we can look at what happens between calls. I previously looked at energetic techniques that can be employed so as to maintain one's optimum energetic level during a shift, but as more and more lines come into existence and more and more readers seem to appear on them, so it follows that gaps between calls may also be greater. This creates an opportunity in terms of 'spare-time' that can be used to good effect.

Of course you cannot begin cleaning the house and cooking dinner for that day during your shift. You need to remain focussed on your work and ready to roll at a seconds notice. That can often entail remaining at ones' post, most often from my experience, in front of the computer. This brings us nicely to the possibility of using 'down-time' between calls for the furtherance and pursuit of our career.

Everyone likes something new and like kids in a sweetie shop, your callers will love to try a 'bit of this and bit of that', both in terms of different readers and the skills and abilities they have. The chances are that you will have one speciality in your arsenal of ammunition with which to strike your callers and help them. There are a great many psychic skills out there and an ever-expanding number of ways to use those abilities. If we take the Tarot for example, more and more different decks are continually being produced and all can take time to learn, study and integrate with our established practice. This is to everyone's benefit and we should not ignore the importance and actual necessity of what is known now as 'continuing professional development', in the work and career of the telephone psychic.

So between your calls it is likely you will have a body of time on occasions when your range of activities is limited. This is a prime time when you can be working on the necessary 'C.P.D.' as it is now known. This allows you to expand your knowledge, skills and experience while keeping your mental and emotional focus where it needs to be for the duration of time that you are logged on. Of course you will need to develop the requisite habit of being able to switch to giving a great reading as soon as the telephone rings, but with a little practice this will soon come and from experience I can tell you that is not a problem.

Next comes the choice of what exactly what you study or work on between these calls. As already mentioned, for Tarot readers a new or alternative deck (there is and seemingly never will be a dearth of decks!) can be studied, simply by placing a deck in front of you and making notes on what comes to you, card by card. You can practice doing 'imaginary' readings with your shiny new deck, imagining you are reading for a celebrity whose in the news (again, never a lack of these!) for whatever crisis or dilemma is apparently happening to them.

This brings us to another lovely opportunity for the Tarotists amongst you. Just as there are an endless production of new decks for you to feast upon, so there are new and divergent spreads with which to read them. These can be gleaned from the internet for no cost and nearly all psychics I know have a goodly number of Tarot books adorning their groaning bookshelves and these seem to all feature the authors 'innovative and revolutionary' spreads. You can experiment with these and this will add to the variety of what you can offer your callers with their many and varied needs. For the more brave and adventurous amongst you, you can even try your hand at creating your own spreads – who knows you may end up writing a book of them! If that doesn't appeal, have a god at (gasp) reading without a spread at all. This is something I personally favour and if you want to find out all about that, you'll have to get the first of my 'Tarot Therapy' series of books – and hopefully then volumes 2 and 3!

Mention of writing a book between your calls is not so silly or far-fetched an idea as you think – indeed some of this very book has been written in such a manner, so if I can, so can you! If writing is not your thing, perhaps reading is and you can avail yourself of the opportunity afforded you between calls to read through that hefty volume of psychic development techniques or Buddhist approaches to meditation you've been promising you will do 'one of these fine days'. If you do choose to devote your downtime to reading it is much the better option for it to be of something akin to your readings, so do try to choose something of a positive, uplifting, spiritual nature rather than the latest horror novel.

We have seen that call downtime is a great opportunity to enhance and develop ones' existing skills, which ultimately benefits you, your callers, the Company you work with and your bank balance! We should also be aware of what we can see as a necessity in the work and career of the (telephone) psychic – that of expanding one's profile with the addition of new abilities and skills. These require some learning, or I feel that your attitude should at least be humble and open enough to accept this in principle – that just because you are already a professional psychic does not mean that you can simply pick up any tool and start using it in a professional capacity.

There is no substitute when it comes to learning new skills, arguably perhaps especially those in the psychic field, which require getting to grips with concepts and practices that may be hitherto unfamiliar. The advent of the internet heralded quite literally a whole new world opening up for us all. There are now some great resources for 'distance learning' which can be done seated at ones' desk between calls. These do not break the bank and the majority will also provide you with some kind of certification. Aside from my own (which you can see www.tarottherapy.co.uk), the most suitable, advantageous and best quality I have seen can be seen equally at - http://www.bsygroup.co.uk/ and https://www.stonebridge.uk.com/

A quick frolic around these sites will soon reveal a number of opportunities with something to tickle your proverbial fancy, whatever your particular psychic tastes are! You can then add to your website profile that you are 'currently studying and will shortly offer' readings using whatever it is. Your callers will see this, ask you about it and will want to try – remember the sweetie shop approach!

The acquisition of new and additional skills is always a good thing to aim for, regardless of how long in the tooth you are when it comes to psychic readings (of any kind really, not just by telephone). Here you can achieve this aim and make excellent and productive, not to mention profitable, use of your available time. Continuing Professional Development should be your norm, in whatever way or shape this occurs.

SEEKING SUPPORT

Part of this can also be the need for some objectivity to your activity! Some and the more forward-thinking, quality conscious amongst them may offer feedback on your calls. This will involve listening to a number of your calls at random (this is not usually done 'live' so you need have no qualms about anyone eavesdropping and even if this facility does exist, you will not be aware of it). There is really an approach required from you now to be open to being heard on each and every one of your calls – you should be saying or doing anything you would not want anyone to hear.

Of course the person listening to and providing feedback on your performance may not be as experienced as you or even actively involved in giving readings themselves – although this would of course be preferable. Much can be gained from the simple fact of their being an objective viewpoint to your calls and one that listens both from your perspective as a reader and the callers standpoint.

When you receive such feedback you do need to be genuinely open to this and approach what is offered to you with all due humility. Even the most accomplished and experienced psychics can improve and this can practice can go a long way to ensuring that you do not become stale and offer less than your best, as your caller always deserves. Of course much is required by way of diplomacy on the part of the reviewer but that is their job, not yours and the ones I know of, myself included, have bags and bundles of practice and tact.

You do not of course have to accept everything that is said as a gospel kind of law to which you must adhere or risk some eternal kind of damnation! However, you can adopt an attitude of 'I can learn from this' however small a nugget of insight and wisdom you may glean from such a session. It is well known in the counselling profession that practising counsellors must seek their own counselling after so many hours of practice, for many good and valid reasons and those same principles operate here.

Some companies may insist on this and this is all for the good. If they do not, they may operate basis of calling just on the odd occasion to review your calls and performance, and if they do not, there are still many good reasons to request this occasionally. This will how willingness on your part, demonstrate your care and professionalism and may set you apart in all god ways from 'the rest'. Of course, and as I often reminded those who were resistant for whatever reason, the end result of such feedback is that your calls can lengthen and you earn more money and since this will be a prime reason for your being there, if you are honest, this can only be a good thing.

How often these 'supervision' sessions occur can chiefly be dependent on how many hours per week you are doing online, or how many readings you give. Just as many professionals do in their chosen field, you may go through a 'dry patch' where something is lacking or you are aware you are not quite hitting the bulls-eye in terms of accuracy, clarity or depth with your psychic information and this is nothing to be ashamed of, or ignored. Indeed, it is seen a sign of strength and positivity if you are willing to look at this, let alone amidst it and furthermore, act on it.

It may be that you find you have a difficulty with a particular 'type' or attitude of callers or subjects they want readings on, or with one kind of Tarot spread or whatever it may be in your chosen speciality. You can note a reading where you know you struggled and were not as good as you either could or should have been and just ask for this to be listened to. Even if you feel everything is going swimmingly well in your readings and all your callers express undying love and devotion to you and ring in droves, you can still benefit from a review and honest, positive, 'constructive criticism'.

TAKE A BREAK

I have mentioned above the issue of how many hours per week you may be doing with your chosen psychic line. This can vary enormously and have different impacts. Of course the more you do the more 'maintenance' will be required to keep you fresh and thriving as you go. This may be something as simple as ensuring you drink a good quantity of water throughout your shift, to keep your energy levels alive and flowing – this is a good practice to acquire just for general health and well-being anyway and one which I heartily recommend.

We have explored the need for objective and constructive criticism above and now we turn our attention to the need for breaks and rest from psychic work. All work we do affects us in different ways. For the psychic the work done primarily has an effect on our own energetic levels and these need to be replenished, so when we next return we are at our best.

The easiest way to examine this is to approach it from a number of hours' viewpoint. Many psychic companies will divide their rota stints into three or perhaps four hour blocks, often with a maximum applied both to one day and a week, this being sensible for different reasons. It can be tempting, especially if your chosen line is not giving you calls that just keep coming, to log yourself on at all times, flit around your house dong this and that and just grabbing your 'phone when it rings' This is not, in my view, the way to give the best kind of reading to a caller when they are presented to you. Fat better to select what you know will be your limit in terms of how many hours and when in the day you know you are at your best to give your best reading. If you doubt this, just put yourself in the place of your caller, who will be paying upwards of £30 for a 20 minute reading from you.

Whilst every good psychic worth their pendulum needs to apply their own individual limit to how many hours they can truly work to their best per day, this also applies on a collective level too, in terms of how many hours per week and indeed per month and year. Whilst it is recognised and understood that you need to make money and sometimes this can necessitate logging for longer than you would normally, or would wish to do, this has to be balanced with the equal need for quality of service.

I have known many a very good telephone psychic who logs on every day of the week to try and achieve their requisite income. Nearly always, they failed. This I feel, was largely due to the resultant dip in quality. First in this comes the fact that callers like variety, different callers call at different times of the day and days of the week. If, each and every time they log on they see the same reader there, something psychologically tells them to avoid them, since they are simply part of the furniture, rather than that special reader they have been after. Paradoxically to what one might expect, logging on every day actually results in less calls rather than more because of this psychological imprint we all have.

Psychically too, we need to have a minimum of one day per week where we are not undertaking any psychic activity at all. It can be very easy, as we are lucky enough as psychics to earn money from what we love to do and are good at, (or this should be the case at least) to want to work, since it does not feel like work to us – it is what we choose to do and is really part of our lifestyle. I have often said that in earning my living in the psychic world generally is 'better than working for a living'! What I mean by this is not that I don't work, (in contrast I work far more hours now than I ever did when I was employed!) but that it does not feel like work. What I have learnt however is the need to rest my psychic muscles and activity for a day per week if I am to operate at the highest standard I am capable of, and that is, and has to be, the target of every psychic who ever gives a reading.

All athletes, of whatever kind, know that part of staying at peak fitness levels is to rest and this also applies to our psychic fitness. It is not that we have to be 'spiritual' all the time and involved constantly and continually with psychic matters – everything is spiritual anyway so this feeling is a fallacy and will only lead to overload.

This can be a very real condition, that of psychic overload. If we do not take time to rest and recuperate at a psychic level, we will become drained. However brilliant we are a applying all the strategies and techniques we know maintain us, as we should always do, over time this work is draining and debilitating if we do not take a break from it occasionally. This may simply be giving ourselves a day off per week and perhaps a two-week break once per year.

I have known readers who suffer continual, non-specific illness – aches, pains, colds, etc. – due to not taking a break. One I had insisted, as my role required, that they do so, they then returned refreshed and raring to go and came out of the starting blocks at a rate of knots, soon notching up many a happy (and returning) caller. I've made this point in different ways now and highlighted different aspects around this issue, so it's high time I took a break!

GET BRANDED

Given that we can now look at telephone psychism as a career option and therefore as a business, it is worthwhile to see yourself as a marketable 'brand', along with all the other brands that swamp our hearts and minds in the big wide world these days. Whilst we do this in the telephone psychic world via your website profile on the companies' website you work with, there are other options available to you that you can also make use of to help promote your individual brand.

A new phenomenon rife not just amongst telephone psychics, but seemingly the whole world (and his wife!) is social media. Whatever we may think of this – and I am among those who remain completely befuddled as to why people would want to put photos of their dinner for the rest of the world to see – it does offer wonderful and effective opportunities for 'networking' to use another somewhat nauseatingly trendy term.

Leaving aside the rather tempting tendency to use this opportunity to highlight the shallowness and ridiculousness of social media in general, I will instead focus on the uses that can be made by the telephone psychic.

What should be made clear from the outset however is a danger – and not just that of sinking deeply into the mire of mundane tedium social media seeks to enmesh you in! Rather the danger here is that you, unwittingly or otherwise, find yourself removed from your chosen company due to stealing their callers.

From a legal standpoint, if you are seen (and most companies will check these days) to be attempting to get any of your callers to contact you privately or by any means other than through their lines, chat facility and so on, this can be classed as corporate theft. The legal system, bastion of capitalism as it necessarily is, does not take kindly to someone stealing anther's potential profit, and is equipped to hand out large fines and worse for such transgressions. That said, there is no law against your being 'on' social media such as 'facebook', 'twitter' et. al. – it is what you do there that matters.

On the assumption that you would rather not be subjected to legal investigation and being branded a fraud across the industry, we should instead look at how you can make a good and positive, acceptable use of your network of 'friends' who tag along on your social media joyride. It is after all, an excellent means of 'spreading the word' and attracting more callers to your cause. The operations of many telephone psychic companies are increasingly leaning towards providing you a platform from which to run your business, or at least the part of your work that this covers.

It is worthwhile then setting up your own facebook page that is titled by your chosen online name and pin number. You can add to this the telephone number and booking information, along with details of cost of calls, so that everything is readily and easily accessible.

You can then post your rota times, say each week, and pop a little post there each time you log on. You can of course add individual messages as they occur to you, to generate interest and ultimately, calls. Given that most of the world is already on facebook, I will not include instructions as to how to set yourself up there, since in all likelihood you already are!

It is also an easy thing to link up your facebook telephone psychic page to a similarly created twitter page. Once done, every time you then post something on facebook, it is automatically 'twittered' (if that is a word!) for all to see.

This also provided a good forum for you to say how much you

enjoyed your readings, at the end of each shift, or a little snippet of information to attract and maintain interest from your 'friends' there. You need to protect the anonymity of your callers of course, so do not mention names or anything that could be used to identify anyone and cause any embarrassment. The best approach here is that if you have any doubt, do not say it. You can also post information to give more detail of how you work, what you do, good experiences you have had online and perhaps even a message to entice someone to call – something along the lines of 'I am being given a message today that someone has real fears about taking a job they've been offered this morning – do call me if you would like a reading on this'. Just ask your guide or whatever method you use to receive something that will help someone who is in need and go from there.

Leaving behind the scintillating world of social media now, you may also look at other ways that you can promote your brand. Although you may work independently of your telephone psychic work, it can be useful to create a separate brand, image or identity just for this aspect of your career. There are many places available on the internet now that allow you to create a website for free. This does not have to be elaborate and feature the 'bells and whistles' possible elsewhere, but something pretty and appealing to look at. This really only need to give the details that someone might want to know in deciding whether or which telephone psychic to call.

This should be a detailed profile, giving your training, development and qualifications and a thorough outline of how you work and your range of skills, with a good explanation of what these are, for the uninformed. You can also add some good quality images of yourself, along with detailed times, day by day of your availability. Of course it may seem like a slim chance that people will find you amidst the masses that are out there these days, but a chance there is. Since it costs nothing to do now, there is absolutely no reason not to do so. Updating your website, along with additions to your social media presence is another great thing you can be doing in the downtime between calls.

Most psychics, along with business people from all walks of life, have a business card. These are also cheaply available via the internet (what isn't!) and once done can be given out freely everywhere you go. Of course you may choose to integrate your telephone work with your other activities in the psychic world, but keeping it as a separate brand can set you apart. How and if you choose to do this is a matter for each individual, I am simply sowing seeds and planting ideas, to use a couple of suitable gardening analogies!

CONCLUSION

We have gone from humble beginnings as a fledgling and trembling psychic next to a telephone line to a branded, recognised expert with the world at their fingertips. No doubt there will be a need to continue to evolve with the evolution of the telephone psychic world itself and that is at it should be.

What is perhaps most important at this stage is the manner in which we carry out our work on a day to day basis. From an energetic point of view, we create our own reality, so if you are putting it out there, it will come back. Be clear and work with a positive expectation about this. This applies both in terms of the manner in which you project yourself and your brand as well as the number and quality of calls that you will receive.

One thing from a spiritual perspective that I have found especially useful is that of the requests and offer I make to my guide before each and every shift. This is to offer myself as available and to be used for the time I am logged on to the line, by those that need me. I then ask my guide to present those callers to me that it is right that I should speak with, for whatever reason. This seems to have the effect of reducing drastically the number of callers who I cannot connect with, or those that are aggressive and nasty.

This also has the demonstration and effect that I am in the correct place of availability and service, whilst also maximising my earnings opportunities from this correct standpoint. Of course this does mean that each and every shift I receive non-stop calls that all last the full 20 minute or available time-span and that every caller is full of sweetness, light and love. What it does mean is that most of the calls I do get are from those who are open to the information I am able to give them, are responsive to it and perhaps most importantly, able to get some use from their reading to help themselves and their lives.

Much as your reason for being a telephone psychic may well be to make money, and there is nothing wrong with this at all, what should also be remembered all the time, is that what we do affects real people, with real lives, real issues, situations and problems and that the readings we give them could make a real difference to their experience of life. This is a real privilege and it is my hope that you get to experience the full measure of this.

TAROT THERAPY PRODUCTS

Steve Hounsome produces a range of products and services, which are detailed below –

TAROT THERAPY TRAINING

There are three courses available, for those wishing to train as a Tarot Therapist –

- **INTRODUCTION** – For the complete beginner
- **CERTIFICATE** – For those wanting to read professionally for others
- **DIPLOMA** - For those wanting to develop their existing knowledge and ability

TAROT THERAPY READINGS, PAST LIVES, MEDIUMSHIP

Steve is available for readings either in person in Dorset, England, by 'phone or by email.

PERSONAL, PSYCHIC & SPIRITUAL DEVELOPMENT

Steve has produced a range of meditations and exercises for personal, psychic and spiritual development. These are available as cd's or as downloads from the website.

MEDITATION, PSYCHIC DEVELOPMENT & TAROT STUDY GROUPS

Steve runs groups in all the above subjects, as well as holding a series of workshops throughout the year, in Dorset, England.

Full details of all the above are available at Steve's website –

www.tarottherapy.co.uk

You can also email Steve at –

steve@tarottherapy.co.uk